D251 BLOCK 3 UNITS 8 AND 9
SOCIAL SCIENCES: A SECOND LEVEL COURSE
D251 ISSUES IN DEAFNESS

CONSTRUCTING DEAFNESS

PAINTING ON COVER AND TITLE PAGE BY TREVOR LANDELL

INTRODUCTION TO BLOCK 3

UNIT 8
THE SOCIAL CONSTRUCTION OF DEAFNESS

PREPARED FOR THE COURSE TEAM BY
TIM DANT AND SUSAN GREGORY

UNIT 9
DEAF PEOPLE AS A MINORITY GROUP: THE POLITICAL PROCESS

PREPARED FOR THE COURSE TEAM BY
PADDY LADD AND MARY JOHN

The Open University

THIS COURSE HAS BEEN PRODUCED WITH FUNDING
FROM THE DEPARTMENT OF HEALTH

D251 Core Course Team

ANNE DARBY Diploma Placements Officer, Faculty of Social Sciences

SUSAN GREGORY Senior Lecturer in Psychology, Faculty of Social Sciences (Course Team Chair)

YVONNE HOLMES Secretary, Faculty of Social Sciences

LINDA JANES Course Manager, Faculty of Social Sciences

GEORGE TAYLOR Lecturer in Interdisciplinary Social Sciences, Faculty of Social Sciences

Other Open University Contributors

JULIET BISHOP Research Fellow in Social Sciences, Faculty of Social Sciences

DEBBIE CROUCH Designer

TIM DANT Research Fellow in Health and Social Welfare, Continuing Education

VIC FINKELSTEIN Senior Lecturer in Health and Social Welfare, Continuing Education

GERALD HALES Research Fellow, Institute of Educational Technology

FIONA HARRIS Editor

KEITH HOWARD Graphic Artist

MARY JOHN Senior Lecturer in Psychology, Faculty of Social Sciences

VIC LOCKWOOD BBC Producer

KEN PATTON BBC Producer

ALISON TUCKER BBC Producer

External Consultants

LORNA ALLSOP Centre for Deaf Studies, University of Bristol

LARAINE CALLOW Consultant in Deafness

MARY FIELDER National Council of Social Workers with Deaf People

GILLIAN M. HARTLEY Teacher, Thorn Park School, Bradford

LYNNE HAWCROFT Royal National Institute for the Deaf

JIM KYLE Centre for Deaf Studies, University of Bristol

PADDY LADD London Deaf Video Project

CARLO LAURENZI National Deaf Children's Society

CLIVE MASON Presenter, BBC 'See Hear'

RUKHSANA MEHERALI Educational Psychologist, Royal School for the Deaf, Derby

DOROTHY MILES Writer, Lecturer and Poet

BOB PECKFORD British Deaf Association

CHRISTINE PLAYER Tutor Adviser

SHARON RIDGEWAY National Council of Social Workers with Deaf People

JANICE SILO Teacher of the Deaf, Derbyshire

External Assessors

MARY BRENNAN Co-director, MA and Advanced Diploma in Sign Language Studies, University of Durham

MALCOLM PAYNE Head of Department of Applied Community Studies, Manchester Polytechnic

Sign Language Interpreters

BYRON CAMPBELL

ELIZABETH JONES

KYRA POLLITT

LINDA RICHARDS

The Open University
Walton Hall, Milton Keynes
MK7 6AB

First published 1991

Copyright © 1991 The Open University

All rights reserved. No part of this publication may be reproduced, stored in a retrieval system or transmitted, in any form or by any means, without written permission from the publisher or a licence from the Copyright Licensing Agency Limited. Details of such licences (for reprographic reproduction) may be obtained from the Copyright Licensing Agency Ltd of 33–34 Alfred Place, London WC1E 7DP.

Designed by the Graphic Design Group of the Open University

Printed in the United Kingdom by The Open University

ISBN 0 7492 0054 5

This publication forms part of the Open University course D251 Issues in Deafness. If you have not enrolled on the course and would like to buy this or other Open University material, please write to Open University Educational Enterprises Ltd, 12 Cofferidge Close, Stony Stratford, Milton Keynes MK11 1BY, United Kingdom. If you wish to enquire about enrolling as an Open University student, please write to the Admissions Office, The Open University, P.O. Box 48, Walton Hall, Milton Keynes MK7 6AB, United Kingdom.

Introduction to Block 3

In Block 3 we widen our approach still further and analyse deafness from a theoretical perspective, as a socially constructed category. This block also considers in more detail the different implications of considering Deaf people as a linguistic minority, or as a disabled group, and examines Deaf politics and the politics of deafness.

Unit 8, on 'constructing deafness', draws together much of the course studied so far in contrasting the various constructions of deafness, including that of Deaf people themselves and the Deaf community, that of the institutions of education and social work, and those of fictional accounts such as novels and films. Reader Two, *Constructing Deafness*, is reviewed in parallel with this unit.

Unit 9 provides a further analysis by taking a Deaf perspective on these constructions and a major part of this unit is written from the viewpoint of an individual Deaf person. Here the activist's view is contrasted with the perspective of the political analyst and the tensions between these two approaches are examined.

The theme of politics and deafness is considered further in Unit 10, where political demonstrations by Deaf people are described. This is examined in the context of raising questions about how the future might be for Deaf people. Thus, in addition to politics, the role of artistic expression and the increasing impact of technology are also considered.

Unit 8 The Social Construction of Deafness

prepared for the course team by Tim Dant and Susan Gregory

Contents

continued

Associated study materials

See Study Guide. (Note: Most of the reading involves reviewing articles read previously.)

D251 Issues in Deafness

Unit 1   *Perspectives on Deafness: An Introduction*

Block 1   Being Deaf

Unit 2   *The Deaf Community*

Unit 3   *British Sign Language, Communication and Deafness*

Unit 4   *The Other Deaf Community?*

Block 2   Deaf People in Hearing Worlds

Unit 5   *Education and Deaf People: Learning to Communicate or Communicating to Learn?*

Unit 6   *The Manufacture of Disadvantage*

Unit 7   *Whose Welfare?*

Block 3   Constructing Deafness

Unit 8   *The Social Construction of Deafness*

Unit 9   *Deaf People as a Minority Group: The Political Process*

Unit 10   *Deaf Futures*

Readers

Reader One: Taylor, G. and Bishop, J. (eds) (1990) *Being Deaf: The Experience of Deafness*, London, Pinter Publishers.

Reader Two: Gregory, S. and Hartley, G.M. (eds) (1990) *Constructing Deafness*, London, Pinter Publishers.

Set Books

Kyle, J. and Woll, B. (1985) *Sign Language: The Study of Deaf People and Their Language*, Cambridge, Cambridge University Press.

Miles, D. (1988) *British Sign Language: A Beginner's Guide*, London, BBC Books (BBC Enterprises). With a chapter by Paddy Ladd.

Videotapes

Video One   *Sandra's Story: The History of a Deaf Family*

Video Two   *Sign Language*

Video Three   *Deaf People and Mental Health*

Video Four   *Signs of Change: Politics and the Deaf Community*

Aims and objectives

The aim of this unit is to introduce the notion of social construction, and to illustrate how deafness is constructed in a number of different contexts.

After studying this unit you should be able to:

1   Understand what is meant by social construction.
2   Contrast different constructions of deafness in the Deaf community, professional discourses and popular understandings.
3   Be aware of the differing implications of these various constructions for Deaf people.

Study guide

This is a substantial unit and some of the ideas are complex. However, you will find that it also pulls together much of the course content to date. While there is a considerable amount of reading, much of it from Reader Two, you will find that most of it is the re-reading of articles already studied. In some sense this unit is a guide to Reader Two and you will find it relevant to read both the Introduction and the section introductions in the Reader as well as the individual articles. You will also find that most sections in this unit relate specifically to particular sections in the Reader.

We suggest that you divide up the work as follows:

Week one

Unit sections:
Introduction
1 'Establishing a Deaf identity'
2 'Popular conceptions of deafness'
Reader Two:
Introduction
Article 1.1 by Carol Padden and Tom Humphries
Section 2 *Defining the Deaf Community*
Section 8 *Deafness Portrayed: Deaf People in Film and Fiction*
Set books:
J. Kyle and B. Woll, *Sign Language: The Study of Deaf People and Their Language*, Chapter 1.
D. Miles, *British Sign Language: A Beginner's Guide*, Chapter 2 by Paddy Ladd.

Week two

Unit sections:
3 'Science and medicine'
4 'Deafness as deficiency'
5 'Education'
Reader One:
Article 2 by Kathy Robinson
Article 3 by Lorraine Fletcher
Reader Two:
Article 3.1 by Stephen Quigley and Peter Paul
Article 3.2 by Jim Kyle
Article 4.2 by William Noble
Article 5.1 by British Association of Teachers of the Deaf
Article 5.5 by Wendy Lynas, Alan Huntington and Ivan Tucker
Article 5.6 by Lionel Evans
Article 5.7 by Miranda Llwellyn-Jones
Article 5.9 by Wendy Lynas
Article 5.10 by Tony Booth
Article 5.11 by Susan Gregory and Juliet Bishop

Week three

Unit sections:
6 'Social policy'
7 'Language, knowledge and power'
Reader Two:
Article 1.2 by Nora Groce
Article 7.2 by George Taylor
Article 7.3 by David Parratt and Brenda Tipping

Section 7 in the unit draws together many of the issues addressed—you should have time in the third week to use this section to review the unit as a whole.

Introduction

'I never knew I was deaf until I first entered school' (Howard). 'I never knew I was hearing until I was six' (Joe). These two quotations are taken from the first chapter of *Deaf in America* by Carol Padden and Tom Humphries (Padden and Humphries, 1988a). The chapter itself is entitled 'Learning to be Deaf'. It illustrates how being deaf or hearing for a child from a Deaf family only becomes an issue when contrasted with other possibilities that make being deaf or hearing significant.

Howard realized he was deaf when he went to school. He already knew the sign DEAF, but at school the sign was used in a different way. The teachers used it to mean 'them' whereas for Howard it had always been used to mean 'us'. Joe, like other hearing children in Deaf families, had no reason to think he was different from the rest of his family. The second part of the above quotation reads: 'I never suspected I was in any way different from my parents and siblings'. Hearing people might wonder *why* he was not aware of any difference. Surely he noticed sounds that the rest of the family did not? But even if he were to respond to a noise that the others missed he would have no reason to explain such an event. The same chapter tells of Sam Supalla, who tried to have a conversation with the girl next door and wondered why she could not communicate with him. At a later time his mother explained to him that some people were hearing and they communicated by moving their mouths.

◀ Reading
These examples are given in Article 1.1, 'Learning to be Deaf' by Carol Padden and Tom Humphries in Reader Two. You should read this now and consider the significance of the title. ◀

Padden and Humphries, in the introduction to their book, say that their aim is to write about the positive aspects of Deaf people's lives, rather than the identity that has been imposed upon them by hearing people, an identity usually constructed around the notion of the absence of hearing and the need to make good the 'deficiency'. The title, *Learning to be Deaf*, emphasizes that becoming 'Deaf' is a process arising from the ways in which deafness is talked about within a culture and how the person understands and relates to these.

In this unit we will refer to these different ways of talking about things as 'discourses'—they might be seen as topics, themes or issues around which talk or writing is focused. For example, some accounts of deafness are related to an understanding of the Deaf community; then there are the popular notions of deafness depicted in films and literature; and there are medical, educational and social policy accounts of deafness. In the sections that follow we will look at all of these different discursive contexts and present some of the ways in which deafness is talked about in them: what is meant by the use of words like 'deafness' can be different in different discourses, although there are often connections between them.

The ways in which deafness is constructed in different discourses is important for understanding the way that a culture as a whole defines deafness, as well as what individual people might understand by the term. The link between personal identity and discourse is not specific to the issue of deafness, of course. A recent book, *Texts of Identity*, examined, among others, discourses around the themes of terrorism, lesbianism, and being a patient (Shotter and Gergen, 1989). One of the book's editors, John Shotter, has said elsewhere:

> ... our accounts of ourselves must be clearly situated in the world to which we owe our being as we understand it, in the world of our everyday social life ... our understanding and our experience of our reality are constituted for us very largely by the ways in which we must talk in our attempts to account for the things and events within it.
>
> (Shotter, 1984)

In this unit we will look at those ways of talking which contribute to Deaf people's understanding of themselves as Deaf, and the way in which the whole idea of deafness is constructed within our society. Later in the unit we will explore what we mean by 'social construction' and how the phrase is used in sociological accounts. Rather than begin with the theory, we felt that the unit would be more accessible if we began by looking at different ways in which deafness is talked about and referred to, although it might be helpful just to try to summarize what we are referring to when we write of the 'social construction of deafness':

> *What deafness means is defined not by individual experience of it but through experiences shared through language and practical social situations. These experiences include both the first-hand experiences of those who are deaf and the experiences of those who come into contact with people who are deaf. There is no one true, original meaning of deafness; there are rather, meanings created in various social contexts, that have different effects on the way both deaf and hearing people are encouraged to feel about deafness, about the way deaf people are treated and about the way their situation is located in the culture as a whole.*

The social construction of deafness is a theme that underlies many of the issues raised already in this course. Our aim in this unit is to explore in greater depth the processes of social construction as they relate to deafness. Our approach will be to look at a series of discursive contexts in which issues relating to deafness are raised. It is through these various accounts of deafness that deafness is defined: these discursive contexts give it a meaning for all of us and affect how we understand it.

1 Establishing a Deaf identity

1.1 Deaf community and culture

In recent years there has emerged a conscious attempt by Deaf people to assert what it is to be Deaf, to define deafness themselves. In this section, we shall attempt to examine how deafness is constructed by Deaf people. As hearing writers our view is that of outsiders, as it is in many of the perspectives we shall be examining in this unit. However, we shall make use of the available writings by Deaf people in discussing this topic. Recent years have seen the rejection by the Deaf community of 'hearing' notions of deafness in terms of loss, and a discourse around positive Deaf identities and Deaf culture has developed instead. This has included discussion of who is Deaf and what it means to belong, and who does or does not belong, to the Deaf community. Discourse around the notion of the Deaf community draws on the history, culture, humour and values of that community, all of which are different in emphasis from those of the hearing world.

◄ Reading
Now that you are reaching the end of the course you should consider again the notion of the Deaf community. Compare your own ideas with those in Unit 2; the articles in Reader Two, Section 2; Chapter 2 by Paddy Ladd in the set book by Miles, *British Sign Language;* and Chapter 1 in the set book by Kyle and Woll, *Sign Language: The Study of Deaf People and Their Language.* ◄

◄ Comment
Common features will have appeared in these descriptions together with inconsistencies. The articles differ in their views on whether hearing people can be seen as part of the Deaf community and whether members have to be proficient in the use of sign language. The question also arises as to whether being part of the Deaf community automatically implies being part of Deaf culture in the way in which Carol Padden in Article 2.4 distinguishes between the two. However, the essential feature is that the criterion for who is Deaf is not audiological and based on hearing loss, but rather is based on attitude to deafness and on language use. Thus the criterion is positive, of espousing positive values rather than negative, of being not hearing. ◄

A definition of 'Deaf' which depends on attitude rather than on hearing loss can be problematic, as logically it can include those who are not deaf in the audiological sense. This raises questions as to who decides who is Deaf and whether or not an individual can elect to be Deaf. Are there, as Kannapell suggests, degrees of membership of the Deaf community?

> A deaf person who is in the core of the Deaf community is considered to be 'culturally deaf'. The more culturally deaf a person becomes, the further he or she moves into the core of the Deaf community.
> (Kannapell, 1982)

Such problems of defining group membership are not specific to the Deaf community. Interesting parallels can be found in definitions of who is lesbian, for example. Jeffreys (1989) suggests that one of the problems in writing lesbian history is that in the past lesbians have rarely been identified as such and there is difficulty in deciding who is or is not lesbian. It is an issue on which lesbians themselves disagree. They ask:

> Do we define 'lesbian' as applying only to women who had genital connections with each other? Or only to women who prioritized their love for women and made it central to their existence, refusing to organize their lives around men as society demands? It would be difficult to insist on a narrow sexual definition for lesbians in history because we have so little evidence as to whether they 'did it'.
>
> (Lesbian History Group, 1989)

The distinction created here between a physical and an attitudinal definition has obvious parallels in specifying what it is to be Deaf.

A consequence of defining deafness within the Deaf community as a cultural rather than an audiological category has been the emergence of the Deaf/deaf distinction which we have attempted to use throughout this course. As you will have seen, such usage is not without its problems.

ITQ

Consider the way in which the Deaf/deaf distinction constructs the Deaf community. What are the implications of making this distinction?

◀ Comment

The distinction carries the implication that Deaf people constitute a specific cultural group in an equivalent way to French people or Jamaican people. However, the distinction between the audiological use of the word deaf and the cultural one is not always clear and this can create difficulties, particularly with respect to deaf children as it is not always clear where they fit in. Moreover, to some deaf people it has implied that there is an élite Deaf, set apart from others who are not really Deaf. ◀

In addition, the establishment of Deaf culture with its own values is not without problems for those wishing to identify with it. Personal attributes valued in a hearing culture may not be the same in a Deaf world, where what counts or is significant is construed in a different way. Padden, reporting on a study she carried out with Markowicz, points out that conflict is experienced by:

> ... deaf people who are going through the process of becoming Deaf and beginning to assimilate the values of Deaf people ... As an example of a conflict, a deaf person may value her speaking ability and may always have spoken when communicating with other people. But now she learns that speaking does not have the same positive value with Deaf people that it has with hearing people. Even though some Deaf people can hear some speech, and some speak well themselves, speaking is not considered usual or acceptable behaviour within the cultural group. The deaf person finds she must change the behaviour she has always considered normal, acceptable, and positive.
>
> (Padden, 1980)

In what ways is it different to identify with a 'linguistic and cultural minority group' from identifying with a 'disabled minority group'? Are there any similarities between the status of the two groups?

◀ Comment
Within a society some linguistic and cultural minority groups are afforded higher status (e.g. those speaking French in Imperial Russia) and some low status (e.g. Asian communities in British society). It could be argued that those with low status are disabled by society. You should reflect upon the reasons for the attribution of status, and the implications of this for the Deaf community. ◀

1.2 Language and cultural identity

One of the critical aspects in establishing the Deaf identity has been the recognition of the language of Deaf people. Deaf people form a specific linguistic group, and thus the use of language by Deaf people and the attitudes held about that language form part of the notions of deafness within society. In particular, the rejection of or failure to recognize the language of a group of people effectively makes that group functionally invisible. The moves to establish British Sign Language as a language were discussed in Unit 3.

Here again there are parallels with feminism and Black power movements. Ngũgĩ wa Thiong'o has described how European languages were imposed on African schools, and thus alienated people from their own culture:

> The effect of the cultural bomb is to annihilate a people's belief in their names, in their languages, in their environment, in their heritage of struggle, in their unity in their capacities and ultimately in themselves. It makes them see their past as one wasteland of non achievement and makes them want to distance themselves from that wasteland. It makes them want to identify with that which is farthest removed from themselves; for instance with other people's languages rather than their own.
>
> (Ngũgĩ, 1986)

The story Ngũgĩ tells of the means by which African languages were suppressed in schools strikes chords with many Deaf people's accounts of their own education in which sign language was prohibited:

> Thus one of the most humiliating experiences was to be caught speaking Gĩkũyũ in the vicinity of the school. The culprit was given corporal punishment—three to five strokes of the cane on bare buttocks—or was made to carry a metal plate around the neck with instructions such as I AM STUPID or I AM A DONKEY. Sometimes the culprits were fined money they could hardly afford. And how did the teachers catch the culprits? A button was originally given to one pupil who was supposed to hand it over to whoever was caught speaking his native tongue. Whoever had the button at the end of the day

would sing out who had given it to him and the ensuing process would bring out all the culprits of the day. Thus children were being turned into witch hunters and in the process were being taught the lucrative value of being a traitor to one's immediate community.

(Ibid.)

You may find parallels between this and some of the accounts in Reader One.

1.3 Constructing a Deaf history

For any minority group, the discovery of its history is important in establishing identity. When the history has been lost it has to be recreated or reconstructed from available evidence. For some years now Deaf people have been trying to reclaim their history which has been obscured by the hearing history of the world. This has been more apparent in the USA but can also be observed in the UK: the British Deaf Association centenary celebrations in 1990 included the publication of books on Deaf history and Deaf culture (Jackson, 1990; Grant, 1990).

A major work in this area is that of Peter Jackson who has documented the history of British Deaf people. In his preface he points out how such history is often hidden in the hearing history of the world:

> There are enough books in existence that detail the achievements of hearing people who have participated in the Deaf world, such as Bulwer, Wallis, Arnold. It is not the intention of this book to add to such a record. It is also the view of this author that some of these 'achievements' have no parity with what was actually achieved. ... The main drawback with so many books about hearing people was that the deaf subjects who made them so famous scarcely got a mention; sometimes there was no mention at all.
>
> (Jackson, 1990)

John Vickery van Cleve and Barry A. Crouch have written about the Deaf community in the USA in their book *A Place of Their Own*, subtitled *Creating the Deaf Community in America*. In their preface they describe the difficulties of putting together such a book:

> This study grew out of a pedagogic need. In 1985 we began designing a course called the 'History of the American Deaf Community', to be offered for the first time in the fall of 1986 at Gallaudet University. That such a course was only then being developed seemed ironic in retrospect. Gallaudet University was more than one hundred years old. ... The 1960s had seen a proliferation of courses in colleges, universities and secondary schools celebrating the history of various other American minorities, ethnic and religious groups and women. Yet in the late 1980s Gallaudet University still did not offer a course that would help its students understand their past.
>
> One reason was the lack of the solid historical research upon which any rigorous course must be constructed. With the exception of Jack

Gannon, author of *Deaf Heritage*, deaf people had neither produced their own histories themselves, nor attracted the attention of hearing scholars. Deafness had for too long been viewed from the perspective of pathology ...

The absence of historical studies about deaf people was also due to characteristics that deaf people shared with other minorities in American history. They have usually been poor, blocked by their hearing loss from the usual avenues to wealth in this society, and they have never held positions of political strength or importance because of their poverty and their small numbers. Thus their history was, and is, devalued. Those who control society write its past and attract the attention of its historians. We realized then that our first objective was to uncover what we could about the experiences of a people who seemingly blend into society and leave no trace when they are gone.

Our early efforts concentrated on finding the documents that would tell us, and our students, how it was that deaf people had created a language and a community that had persisted for two centuries ...

It failed. Documents collected ... were simply too opaque for undergraduate students untrained in documentary analysis ...

Our goal in this text, then has been to bring this historical reality out into the open where it can be understood and examined by deaf and hearing people alike.

(van Cleve and Crouch, 1989)

Thus, as with other minority groups, the history of Deaf people has been hidden and features not recorded. It has not been felt significant to mention that a person was deaf or to trace the activities of a group of Deaf people. In Unit 5 mention was made of research into the role of deaf people in the education of deaf children. One of the difficulties in investigating this area has been that for much of the time it was not recorded whether or not a particular teacher was deaf, and this would only become apparent if there was a particular reason to state this. One of the accounts of a fire at Margate School for the Deaf one weekend night reported that it had been difficult to raise the alarm because all the staff in residence that night were deaf. Yet this was only mentioned with a view to recommending that there should always be a hearing person on the premises at night. Implied in this, however, was a clear indication that the majority of staff at the time were in fact deaf. In the same research, obituaries have been discovered making no mention of the person's deafness, although it was known from other sources that they were deaf (Silo, work in progress).

The whole notion of rediscovering history has parallels in movements in the Black community and the women's movement. Women have described their feeling that their experience is not represented in a history where men are the prime movers. Sheila Rowbotham, the feminist writer, has been concerned with this issue in her work. In one of her early papers she writes: 'We are obscured in the "brotherhood" and the liberation of "mankind". The language which makes us invisible to "history" is not coincidence, but part of our real situation in a society and in a movement we do not control' (Rowbotham, 1972).

Later, she went on to write *Hidden From History: Three Hundred Years of Women's Oppression and the Fight Against It* (1974) in which she argues that women have to view their position in the world through men's eyes. In this she says: 'The modern women's movement has produced an immense popular enthusiasm for women's history as part of the challenge to masculine cultural hegemony. History is part of the way we have been defined by men' (Rowbotham, 1974).

A consequence of an account of the history of a culture which obscures or denies particular groups within it, is that individuals may become marginalized or invisible or represented in terms of stereotypes. The hearing notion of deaf people has been largely one of passivity, with high status being accorded to those who courageously accept their disability. Helen Keller, for instance, is portrayed as an example to us all in the way in which she triumphed over adversity. Yet her political activities, which formed a large part of her life, are hidden from view. Throughout her life, Helen Keller was actively involved in politics and was particularly interested in developments in the Soviet Union. Her socialist activities were such that the FBI kept a file on her. In the 1930s and 1940s she spoke at public meetings against fascism, Hitler and Mussolini. Yet, the popular image of her contains no hint of this activity. There are indications that, at the time, there were attempts to conceal this side of her life. In 1963, her German publisher advised her to cut out all references to Lenin in her autobiography *Midstream* (Keller, 1968). Her socialist articles in the newspapers were marginalized as her critics implied she had been indoctrinated by her teacher, Ann Sullivan, and that the views were not her own. She repudiated this suggestion in an article entitled 'How I Became a Socialist' (Keller, 1913). But how did this come about? Was it not possible to conceive that a deaf person could hold such views and be actively involved in politics? Or was it so incompatible with the construction of deafness at the time to be unthinkable?[1]

A further difficulty in recovering the history of Deaf people is that, because they communicate by sign language, events involving deaf people may not have been recorded. Jackson makes this point in the first chapter of his book:

> A heritage that relies largely on the visual does not have a long history unless it is written about, or painted, or built as a permanent structure and here in lies the greatest difficulty in looking at the history of deaf people for their language—British Sign Language—is a visual gestural language where no written form exists like the Ancient Greek, Latin or any other ancient language.

> (Jackson, 1990)

This is, of course, not specific to Deaf people. There are many groups for whom history has not been recorded in a traditional sense and there is an established tradition of 'oral' history referring to stories handed down by word of mouth. In Deaf culture, of course, the words 'oral history' are inappropriate, and the stories are passed on in sign language. Nevertheless, the basic concept is the same. One of the features of such history is the notion of myth, and Deaf culture also has its myths.

[1] For the information about Helen Keller we are indebted to the article by J.C. Quicke, 'Speaking Out: The Political Career of Helen Keller', in *Disability, Handicap and Society*, vol. 13, no. 2, 1988.

At a personal family level, we have Sandra Smith's story of the cockerel, told on Video One, and discussed in Unit 1. Sandra was telling a story to her child to make sense of deafness, and also to create for the child a history of herself as part of a Deaf family which went back for several generations.

A myth with wider applications is perhaps that which surrounds the Abbé de L'Epée, a priest who organized a school based on sign language, for deaf children in France, in the late eighteenth century. Carol Padden, a Deaf woman, describes its significance:

> The popular version of how Epée came to his calling is still told in dramatic form in deaf clubs throughout France. Described in an account of a trip taken throughout France by myself and my husband (Padden and Humphries, 1988), the story of the Abbé de l'Epée is almost always a preface to an official deaf-club event, to remind visitors such as ourselves of the significance of Epée to Deaf people in France. When these stories are told, it is clear that they are not merely anecdotes, but variations on a stylized folk-tale, to be rendered in heightened, lyrical form. One version, recorded by us at one such event, appears below:
>
> 'The Abbé de l'Epée had been walking for a long time through a dark night. He wanted to stop and rest overnight, but he could not find a place to stay, until at a distance he saw a house with a light. He stopped at the house, knocked on the door, but no one answered. He saw that the door was open, so he entered the house and found two young women seated by the fire sewing. He spoke to them, but they still did not respond. He walked closer and spoke to them again, but they failed again to respond. The Abbé was perplexed, but seated himself beside them. They looked up at him and did not speak. At that point, their mother entered the room. Did the Abbé not know that her daughters were deaf? He did not, but now he understood how they had not responded. As he contemplated the young women, the Abbé realized his vocation.'
>
> The theme of the tale is essentially religious as it draw on motifs of a light at the end of a dark road and a warm fire. At the light Epée is introduced to two deaf women and undergoes a transformation. His transformation was perhaps the most powerful motif of all, one which would acknowledge his role in the formation of a national community of deaf people in France. Officially, Epée founded a school for deaf children but he had also created a community of deaf children who were housed together for most of their formative years, children who would later form a secondary community of adults around the core of the school. In some versions of this tale, Epée is proclaimed the father of sign language, the inventor of the language of deaf people. Although the credit is misplaced—no individual can create a language, only generations of speakers can—Epée is symbolically the catalyst for the formation of a community of deaf people that continues to this day.
>
> (Padden, 1990)

In these acts of reinstating myth and reconstituting history, Deaf people are redefining themselves by rooting themselves in a particular history and culture.

1.4 Constructing Deaf identity

This section has looked at the way Deaf people have constructed their identity through explicit accounts of their culture, through the way in which they have defined themselves, and through their history. As hearing people, we have only been able to present an outsider's view which to us seems to reflect Deaf people's own accounts.

To talk of construction in this context is not to imply something which is artificially created; rather, it is to examine a set of discourses that arises as a group becomes established. As with other minority groups, the Deaf construction of deafness is made in reaction to the majority culture. The article by Padden and Humphries, which you read in conjunction with Section 1.1, indicated how deafness, on a personal level, only became an issue for the individuals described when they were confronted by the hearing world. Likewise, in a more general sense, deafness as described by Deaf people is in contrast to the view put forward by the hearing world. As with other groups, the dominant world view is the baseline against which other views are established. White people, men and heterosexuals, for example, do not define themselves or their culture, but Black people, women and homosexuals each define themselves in terms of the dominant groups. You were introduced to the notion of the 'Other' in Unit 4 in the more specific context of the Deaf community. You may find it useful to go back and re-read the first five paragraphs of the Introduction to that unit, paying particular attention to the quotation from de Beauvoir.

2 Popular conceptions of deafness

2.1 Deafness in newspaper articles and fiction

For most of the course so far we have been concerned with a Deaf perspective on deafness or professional discourses. However, there is another view of deafness which must be taken into account in examining the social construction of deafness and that is the popular or lay view, which was introduced in Unit 1. There you were asked to look at the popular perception of deafness by interviewing people about their understanding of deafness, and looking at how deaf people were portrayed in newspaper articles. You also considered the role of deaf people in fiction.

◀ Activity 1

In Unit 1 you were asked to keep a record, as you went through the course, of deaf characters in fiction. You should now review these, addressing the following questions:

1   Are they talking about Deaf or deaf people?
2   Are the images of deaf people presented in the context of a hearing world, or of a deaf world?
3   Are there particular stereotypes that emerge?
4   Contrast the realistic with the non-realistic images. What makes them different?
5   Why is there a deaf person there? What point is being made? What function does he or she serve in the story? ◀

◀ Reading
You should now read Article 8.1, 'Deafness in Fiction' by Susan Gregory in Reader Two.

If possible you should try and obtain at least one of the fictional accounts Gregory describes and read it for yourself, though you should not delay your work on this unit in order to do so. ◀

In her article, Gregory suggests that deafness is used in fiction as a device to comment on aspects of the hearing world. The characters appear to serve the needs of hearing plots and rarely raise issues about Deaf people themselves. Because Deaf people are portrayed individually and in the context of hearing people, nothing emerges about the Deaf community or Deaf culture. Also, because they are presented in isolation they often communicate little, thus they can be used by other characters in the plot in any way they wish. Gregory suggests that 'studying deaf characters in fiction thus tells us remarkably little about deafness itself, but does tell us something about misconceptions which may influence popular notions of deafness.'

2.2 Deafness in film, drama and television

◀ Reading
You should now read Article 8.2, 'Hollywood Speaks: Deafness and the Film Entertainment Industry' by John S. Schuchman in Reader Two. ◀

Schuchman makes similar points to those made by Gregory with regard to the stereotyped deaf characters and the lack of recognition of sign language or the Deaf community, and he also argues that deaf people largely serve as devices on film to move the plot along.

It is further clear from this analysis that there was a time in film production when deafness in actors was irrelevant. In the days of the silent movies deaf and hearing people were both part of the acting profession. Deafness only became an issue with the advent of talking pictures. The startling consequence here was that because deaf people could not play hearing people, deafness came to be seen as a major handicap and deaf people were considered unable to play deaf people either. It seemed that hearing people were better at acting deaf than were deaf people, that hearing people were the experts on how deaf people should be—or that the hearing view of the world dominated in such a way that it became the only acceptable view. At the time of writing this unit, however (June, 1990), there have been several examples of deaf characters being played by deaf people themselves.

This issue is, of course, not specific to deafness. In two recent films which have been major box office successes the leading characters have had disabilities, and in both cases they were played by established actors. In *Rainman*, Dustin Hoffman played the autistic man, and in *My Left Foot*, Daniel Day-Lewis played Christie Brown, who was severely disabled by cerebral palsy. Both these films were accompanied by articles and interviews with the actors describing the work involved in developing their characters: the hours of observation and practice. But should these characters have been played by people with the portrayed disability? Could they have been? If you feel that people with disabilities should always be played by actors with these disabilities, what implications does this have for the rights of disabled people to play able-bodied parts?

With regard to deaf people playing deaf characters, an interesting logistical situation is discussed by Schuchman—that while it is possible to have one deaf person because the hearing people can speak or interpret for them, having more than one, so there are two deaf people signing together, is very rare, as it is seen as difficult to show what they are saying.

ITQ

Does this tell us something about notions of sign language? (After all, we expect foreign spoken languages to be subtitled.)

Probably the most famous play in recent years with deaf characters has been *Children of a Lesser God* (Medoff, 1982). This was an award-winning play, and later, as a film, won an Oscar for its starring actress. It is an excellent example of the point mentioned above concerning a single deaf person with a hearing person who voices both their own signing and that of the deaf part. In the stage version in particular, the male lead was seen as a major undertaking that required speaking in both roles.

The play is about the relationship between a deaf woman and a hearing man, and, although it received major acclaim, many in the Deaf community expressed reservations. One of the questions that arises is whether the play is really about deafness or whether the situation depicted is being used as a vehicle through which to explore the hearing world and ideas about communication and marriage. The following quotations from the last act of the play may help you to decide. James is the hearing man and Sarah the Deaf woman. They are by now married. The first part of the quotation attributed to Sarah and James means that this is Sarah's speech which she signs and James voices:

Sarah and:
James:
For all my life I have been the creation of other people. The first thing I was ever able to understand was that everyone was supposed to hear but I couldn't and that was bad. Then they told me everyone was supposed to be smart but I was dumb. Then they said oh, no, I wasn't permanently dumb, only temporarily, but to be smart I had to become an imitation of the people who had from birth everything a person has to have to be good: ears that hear, mouth that speaks, eyes that read, brain that understands. Well, my brain understands a lot; and my eyes are my ears; and my hands are my voice; and my language, my speech; my ability to communicate is as great as yours. Greater, maybe, because I can communicate to you in one image an idea more complex than you can speak to each other in fifty words. For example, the sign 'to connect', a simple sign—but it means so much more when it is moved between us like this. Now it means to be joined in a shared relationship, to be individual yet as one. A whole concept just like that. Well, I wanted to be joined to other people, but for all my life people have spoken for me: 'She says'; 'she means'; 'she wants'. As if there were no 'I'. As if there were no one in here who could understand. Until you let me be an individual, an 'I', just as you are, you will never truly be able to come inside my silence and know me. And until you can do that, I will never let myself know you. Until that time, we cannot be joined. We cannot share a relationship.

(Silence)

And from later in the same scene:

James:
Until you speak—Okay, you wanna play that one—fine with me. Goddamn right. You want to be independent of me, you want to be a person in your own right, you want people not to pity you, you want them to understand you in the very poetic way you describe in your speech as well as the plain old, boring way normal people understand each other, then you learn to read my lips and you learn to use that little mouth of yours for something besides eating and showing me you're better than hearing girls in bed. Come on, read my lips. What am I saying? Say what I'm saying. What am I saying?

(Sarah starts to sign something. He pins her arms. The rest of this is unsigned)

Shut up. You want to talk to me, then you learn my language. Did you get that? Of course you did. You've probably been reading lips perfectly for years; but it's a great control game, isn't it? You can cook, but you can't speak. You can drive and shop and play bridge but you can't speak. You can even make a speech but you still can't do it alone. You always have to be dependent on someone, and you always will for the rest of your life until you learn to speak. Now come on I want you to speak to me. Let me hear it. Speak. Speak. Speak.

(She erupts like a volcano in speech. She doesn't sign)

(Medoff, 1982)

You need to decide for yourself whether this is a hearing or Deaf perspective on deafness. Perhaps a telling point emerged when the play was filmed because it was edited in such a way as to make it inaccessible to Deaf people. The signing was either off screen or too distant to be read for much of the time. The film was not thus intended to be viewed by Deaf people.

Klobas (1988) in his book *Disability Drama in Television and Film* gives a comprehensive list of the deaf characters portrayed in television as well as in film. Interestingly, he starts his section on deafness with a discussion about the inclusion of deaf people in a book which is, in the first place, about *disability*. He concludes his first paragraph by saying: 'Inclusion here is a concession to the mainstream audience who imagine being deaf is the same as using a wheelchair or being blind. They are wrong'.

From this book, it seems that one of the first television programmes with a deaf character was an episode of *Bonanza*, 'Silent Thunder', transmitted in the USA in December 1960. A little deaf girl was taught sign language by the hero, Joe Cartwright, from a book! She had been rejected by her father, who felt he was to blame for her deafness. When she learnt to sign that she loved her father, he accepted her and asked to be taught the sign for 'daughter'. Klobas comments ' "Silent Thunder" was routine, played for all the drama it could drum up'. Klobas describes a wide range of programmes up to 1986, which illustrates interestingly how many television series have, at one time or another, included a deaf character (e.g. *Magnum, Murder She Wrote, MASH, Little House on the Prairie*). However, as in fictional accounts, deaf characters in television series are often treated in a trivial way, to further the main plot. Klobas makes the point that the frequent emphasis on the deaf person learning to speak in the story suggests that the makers of these programmes see speech as the only important means of communication and that they fail to recognize the value of sign language for the Deaf community. The Deaf community itself and its culture are rarely portrayed or even alluded to. Deaf people are also rarely portrayed as having personalities in their own right, and more often serve to illustrate the development of hearing people.

Recent portrayals of deafness on television in the UK have used a particular means to lessen the need for characterization. Two recent examples (at the time of writing) have been on *Brookside*, a Channel 4 soap opera, and *Prisoner Cell Block H*, an Australian soap opera. In *Brookside* a major character goes to work as an assistant in a school for deaf children, and in *Prisoner Cell Block H* the daughter of a prisoner gives birth to a deaf daughter, who is interestingly diagnosed at birth, an event almost unknown in the real world. Both these examples of deafness are included to illustrate aspects of the main characters in the drama. It is interesting that in both cases the deafness is portrayed in children who need little or no characterization compared to adults. Both situations give rise to clichéd treatment—consider, for instance, the line in *Prisoner Cell Block H*: 'They can do wonderful things these days'.

2.3 Conclusion: reflecting on constructing deafness?

Why should all these portrayals be so important or interesting? It is because they do not simply reflect but also construct a view of deafness. If such constructions perpetuate a view of deaf people as mysterious, as inaccessible, or as victims, this may have a consequence for deaf people. They may find this view imposed upon them, and their behaviour and personality constructed through these images.

◀ Activity 2
You should reflect upon the possible effect of this on the lives of deaf people and their interactions with hearing people, and on their images of themselves. ◀

3 Science and medicine

3.1 Science as a social practice

Science has long been regarded as a powerful form of knowledge. If the natural world is taken as real, objective and independent of human awareness of it, science is usually seen as the best way of studying that world. In describing this traditional view, originally adopted by the sociology of science, Michael Mulkay writes: 'Science is that intellectual enterprise concerned with providing an accurate account of the objects, processes and relationships occurring in the world of natural phenomena' (Mulkay, 1979).

According to this view, the power of science lies in its apparent ability to reveal the true nature of the world in which we live, using methods of empirical observation. What is important about these methods is that they produce an account uncontaminated by the beliefs, preferences, intentions or prejudices of human beings.

This view of science has been seriously challenged in the last 20 years or so, both by philosophers and by sociologists like Mulkay. They point out that it is impossible to devise methods by which human beings can 'know' things without including the human and social characteristics of the practices involved in knowing. Scientific method is not simply objective but a social accomplishment, a way of doing things that follows rules and patterns of behaviour so that other people are able to understand what is happening. Science is a social practice that involves human beings in a set of relationships (some are the bosses, some control the money and promotions) and routinized activity. These things are unavoidable and yet they influence what scientific knowledge is.

Here is how someone quoted in a recent text by Mulkay describes scientific discovery. The quotation is taken from the comments of a sociologist who was contributing to a discussion about the process of scientific discovery.

Most of the contributors were scientists, but this is how the sociologist summed up his position: 'Thus my sociological theory of discovery must come to terms with the fact that the categorization of a scientific contribution as a discovery is an interpretive and variable accomplishment of those involved' (Mulkay, 1985).

This modern sociological view sees science as a social and interpretive activity. Scientific discovery is not simply a matter of revealing factual truth about the natural world but involves human interaction. This can affect not only what is discovered but also how that discovery is perceived and to what use it might be put. The social, and even the political, interests of those involved will affect how they accomplish the discovery even if they have no intention of allowing any such interest to intrude into the process.

Traditionally, science was seen as a special form of knowledge, distinct and separate from other types of human activity. The specialness of science as knowledge derived from its systematic method of observing the world. Its 'objective' perspective meant that it was regarded as invulnerable to criticism based merely on common-sense understanding. Non-scientific disciplines (history, politics, education, the study of art and literature) are often seen as open to comment and contribution from anyone who cares to express an opinion. But scientific disciplines have techniques of observation, measurement and analysis not available to the lay person. Indeed, the importance of the techniques is that they are *distinct* from the common-sense perspective which is assumed to contaminate understanding with subjective opinion and bias.

The respect accorded to scientific knowledge has given scientists and those connected with science considerable power. The modern view of science, which sees it as a social process like any other, is still largely restricted to groups of sociologists and philosophers. In the main, the wider culture continues to regard scientific knowledge as special and not open to challenge from outside the ranks and institutions of science. As a result, science continues to exercise special power as a form of knowledge— although its potency is being challenged. Wright and Treacher, for example, argue that medical knowledge, with its basis in science, is socially constructed. The perspective they wish to promote:

> ... refuses to regard medicine and technical medical knowledge as pre-given entities, separate from all other human activities. Instead, it is argued, medicine is to be seen as a highly specialized domain of social practice and discourse, the limits and contents of which are themselves set up by wider—but not separate—social practices.
>
> (Wright and Treacher, 1982)

They give as an example the way that physicians in the last century advised middle-class women that higher education or a career would damage their capacity to have children. This view was held by many influential men, including journalists and politicians, but since it came from physicians, who could claim to be men of science, it had a different impact: '... because they were presented as part of a scientifically-based medical discourse; because they could call on the supposed structure of the natural world to justify and reinforce the existing social position of women' (ibid.).

Science has an impact on deafness through two related discursive contexts, those of medicine and technology. The scientific perspective of an empirically observed natural world underlies the medical diagnosis and treatment of deafness as well as the provision of aids to compensate for the deficiency identified in the natural order of the body. We hope that in considering how medicine addresses the issue of deafness, you will reflect on how the social aspects of deafness are often obscured and, perhaps more difficult to see, how the social aspects of medicine are obscured. As you continue through the unit you will notice how the medical discourse provides ideas about deafness that are utilized in other formal and powerful discourses such as those of education and the making of social policy.

Before looking at some medical and other scientifically based accounts of deafness, it is important to counter an impression you may be getting. When we write of the 'social construction' of 'meanings' in 'discourses' we are not suggesting that that is all that deafness is—merely a fabrication built up from what people say or write. The point we are making is that deafness cannot be considered separately from the talk about it. The talk and writing that make up what we have called discourse affect what deafness means in practice, to people who are deaf and to people close to those who are deaf. In taking a social constructionist perspective we are not saying that science is wrong or that there is a better way of studying things. What we are saying is that science and medicine provide one, very valuable, perspective that needs to be considered critically along with others. There has been a tendency, because of the enormous success of science in making sense of the material world, to treat it as above the human social world of political interests and the power of different groups. By understanding the ways in which the scientific perspective is established, maintained and used, it can be treated as one which does not invalidate but rather enhances direct human experience—including that of deaf people.

3.2 Anatomy

At the heart of medicine is a particular way of looking at the human body. It involves seeing what is beneath the skin. For those of us not involved in medicine we have very particular ways of looking at bodies; we expect to see other bodies usually clothed, with views of certain parts of others' bodies (and even our own!) only being exposed by accident. For most of us, the idea of looking inside bodies is strange, perhaps abhorrent, perhaps fascinating.

But the medical profession has developed its skills based on knowledge of the insides of bodies. Its understanding of the human body involves a 'three-dimensional' view of what goes on inside, not only of the shapes of the component parts but how they function and interrelate. It is not surprising, then, that medical books which address otology, audiology and the study of deafness often begin with an account of the anatomy of the ear. Indeed, the anatomy of the ear is quite fascinating and surprising.

◀ Activity 3
When you next go to your local library, see what books there are on deafness and how they are arranged. If you can gain access to a medical library you may like to look through some of the textbooks used by doctors. You should spend no more than an hour on this activity—finding what books there are, skimming through, looking at chapter headings and bits of text that look interesting or important.

You should ask yourself what these books tell you about *deafness*, and what they might tell the different readers to whom they are addressed. ◀

◀ Comment
You may notice the significance given to anatomy and to audiometry in the medically oriented books. These are categories of deafness defined not by how the deafness affects living but by how much hearing loss can be measured and the role that medicine might play in remedying that loss. ◀

What rapidly emerges in looking into the descriptions of the workings of the ear, the accounts by doctors of the functions of the ear and the techniques they use for diagnosis and treatment, is that the field is not about deafness (in spite of the names of the less technical books) but about hearing. The descriptions of the workings of the ear are integrated with accounts of what may go wrong with ears, with the 'pathology' of the hearing system. But doctors have to admit, at least to each other, that they can neither explain completely nor do anything about most cases of deafness. Medicine's concern with hearing rather than with deafness can be seen in this passage:

> Hearing is perhaps man's *(sic)* most important sense, for without it his power to communicate is greatly diminished. It is, after all, this superior ability to communicate that sets man above other animals. Unfortunately, it is frequently affected by *pathology* so that a patient develops a *hearing impairment* which results in a *hearing-disability* … at present there is no specific therapy for most of the pathological conditions that affect the auditory system, the exception being some of those that affect the middle ear.
>
> (Browning, 1986, our emphasis)

3.3 Diagnosis

As you will have read in Unit 6, Section 2, medicine applies a categorization of pathology, of deviance from a norm, known as diagnosis. It can be seen as a translation from the experience of the person (pain, discomfort, lack of hearing) into the language of science in which the subjective takes secondary place to the objective. Wherever possible, diagnosis will draw on objective accounts of the body (measurements: counting of components in blood, audiometric analyses; observation unavailable to the subject: X-rays, the view into the ear). Diagnosis attempts to focus on what is pathological or a departure from the 'normal'. But what counts as normal has to be decided by social processes of debate—it may be different in different places at different times. We will return to the issue of 'normal' hearing in the next section on education and language.

◀ Reading
You should now look at Article 4.2, 'Assessment of Impaired Hearing' by William Noble in Reader Two, on the baselines used in audiometry to test hearing. ◀

In both the professional and the lay medical books on deafness you will find an account of the various clinical and audiological tests that are available to doctors attempting to make a diagnosis. We found a book in our local public library with the title *Deafness: the Facts,* written by someone who is clearly trying to help the reader understand what is going on. The author is a consultant ear, nose and throat surgeon and the book is aimed at those with a hearing problem who have come into contact with the medical services. Having begun with an account of the structure and function of the parts of the ear, he goes straight on to describe the hearing tests that doctors are likely to undertake:

> Most doctors do not bother with the voice tests, and start off the examination of hearing by using a tuning fork test. This does not quantify the degree of the patient's hearing; however, it is extremely valuable in establishing whether the hearing loss originates from the middle or the inner ear.
>
> (Freeland, 1989)

There are a number of things going on here that you should notice. Despite the fact that the book is about 'deafness', the examination is of 'hearing'. The doctor's problem is to find the origin of what is perceived as a 'hearing loss'; the patient is not 'deaf' but someone who has lost their hearing. What emerges as one progresses through the text is that there is a range of tests (pure tone audiometry, tympanometry, electrical response audiometry) that help the doctor to locate the site and extent of hearing loss. They enable him or her to identify those cases for which there is a medical role. This is largely in the area of conductive hearing loss, occurring in the middle ear, and is usually related to fluid, an infection or damage to the bony structures of the middle ear. Removing fluid, inserting grommets, treating infections, and surgical intervention to repair damaged bones are all possible therapies that will make an enormous difference to the lives of people suffering from hearing loss for these reasons.

What the textbooks call sensori-neural deafness, however, is, largely, beyond clinical or surgical intervention. The therapy on offer for this is in the form of a hearing aid or lessons in lip-reading. The claims for lip-reading can be impressive:

> When a child is born partially deaf, he (*sic*) will often learn to lip-read quite spontaneously. Many who are born totally deaf can be taught to lip-read, and one has only to see a few 'orally' successful deaf children to realise how valuable these visual clues to speech can be.
>
> (Ballantyne and Martin, 1984)

No scientifically conducted studies are cited and another authority puts it rather differently: 'It would be encouraging to think that current methods of training in Speech-reading are effective but unfortunately, this has yet to be proved' (Browning, 1986).

The hearing aid is the main solution to what medicine sees as 'deafness'. Where other treatments (including surgery) are on offer, these are often combined with the provision of a hearing aid. The hearing aid is, of course, not an aid for the profoundly deaf but an aid for those who have a hearing loss. More specifically, it is for those whose hearing loss is not complicated by the problem of 'recruitment' which is quite commonly associated with sensori-neural deafness:

> ... the patient with sensori-neural deafness reacts quite differently. He is deafened, not helped, by noise. To him, a sound of low intensity may be barely audible, but a relatively slight increase in the *intensity* of the sound is accompanied by an enormously increased sensation of *loudness*.
>
> (Ballantyne and Martin, 1984)

Medicine has no response to 'deafness' other than to remove mechanical barriers to hearing (fluid, damaged bones) or prescribe hearing aids. The profoundly deaf person is then beyond the help of contemporary medicine. It is easy to see why the cochlear implant attracts so much attention—it gives medicine a much more significant role in the treatment of some deafness.

3.4 Medicine and oralism

It is important to note that there is an alliance between the medical approach to hearing loss and the oralist tradition of education. Both put the emphasis on hearing and stress the vital importance of the auditory channel for communication and learning: medicine pays little attention to manual forms of communication. Ballantyne and Martin, for example, interpret the history of the education of the deaf in terms of oralism. They do refer to manual methods of communication, but even in the 1984 edition of their work, originally published in 1960, they say of manualism:

> It may have a useful role, not only in providing an earlier introduction to language for some handicapped children, but also as a reinforcement for other methods of communication; but the limitations of any sign language lie in its lack of speed and in the narrow cultural context in which it can develop. 'Oralism', or the method of training the deaf to communicate (literally) 'by word of mouth', has now largely replaced the manual method (officially) in nearly all of the Schools for the Deaf and the Partially Hearing in Great Britain.
>
> (Ballantyne and Martin, 1984)

This is far from an antiquated or specialist text. We found it in a medical library in a district general hospital where it is likely to be used by hospital doctors, including paediatricians, GPs, and doctors in training. Freeland's more modern approach directed to a less professional audience is to embrace Total Communication: ' ... which gives the child the opportunity of using all forms of communication to extend language, including speech, formalized gestures, finger spelling, lip reading and writing' (Freeland, 1989).

Browning, whose medical textbook is directed at those with a special interest in otology, does not discuss sign language at all (Browning, 1986). These medical sources all discuss hearing aids and lip-reading but demonstrate little understanding of what sign language is and offer little encouragement for its use. This is in spite of the fact that they have little other than 'diagnosis' to offer the profoundly deaf person, especially those born deaf.

Deafness is not simply about not being able to hear, and in the USA there tends to be a broader view of what deafness entails. Hallowell Davis, for example, follows a medical model in approaching deafness but does at least adopt: '... a social criterion for deafness, namely, that everyday auditory communication is impossible or very nearly so' (Davis, 1978). Although older than the English medical references cited, this general medical textbook not only begins with a definition of deafness that concerns communication, it also includes chapters on manual communication, on the debate over educational methods and about the Deaf community.

◄ Reading
This would be a good point at which to read Article 2, 'The Appointment' by Kathy Robinson, and Article 3, 'Discovery and Diagnosis' by Lorraine Fletcher, in Reader One. These articles will help you to understand the context in which parents are presented with deafness and the possible sources of help. ◄

Doctors are not the only people who define deafness but their authoritative role means that parents of deaf children will take serious note of their definitions (as shown in, for example, the articles by Lorraine Fletcher and Kathy Robinson in Reader One), as will other professions, including social workers for the deaf and teachers of deaf children—not least because they have referred to them people who have already been defined by doctors as deaf.

3.5 Screening

In the early diagnosis of deafness doctors have a slightly different role. Because hearing is so much a part of the process of growing up, identifying that a child has a problem with hearing and responding to it can make an enormous difference to the child's development. If, for example, a treatable form of conductive hearing loss can be spotted early on and treated (e.g. by inserting a grommet in the eardrum of a child with middle ear infection, commonly known as 'glue ear'), the child's access to information through the auditory channel will be improved at a crucial time. Even if there is no treatment, the provision of a hearing aid will enable a child with a certain degree of hearing loss to function as 'hearing' and to learn through speech in the same way as children without a hearing loss.

Of course, babies and very young children cannot report that they have a hearing problem; they are unlikely to be aware of having 'lost' hearing, since they never had it. Hearing is not necessary in order to respond to the environment—babies will smile and gurgle and react to attention whether or not they can hear. But if they do not hear they will not be responding to the sounds and spoken language that could be giving them information about their environment and preparing them for language acquisition.

Currently it is parents, health visitors and general practitioners who provide the most likely guide as to whether a child is responding to aural stimuli or not. Some children 'at risk' of being deaf, including those with a family history of sensori-neural deafness, those whose mothers contracted rubella in early pregnancy and those who had a particularly difficult birth, are likely to be tested with electrical auditory response tests.

Screening for deafness in babies or children will help to identify a problem that may or may not be deafness so that a diagnostic process can begin. Some parents say they wish to know as soon as possible if their child is deaf so that they can get to know him or her better; others say they wish to delay diagnosis as long as possible so that they can get to know their child as a 'normal' child (Gregory, 1976). The rapport that parents develop with a child usually involves a range of auditory communication. But if the parent knows that their child cannot hear they may be inhibited from freely relating to him or her, feeling that they have to avoid cooing and talking to the child. On the other hand, knowing that the child is deaf could perhaps enable parents to concentrate attention on a non-auditory channel of communication—the development of manually coded language.

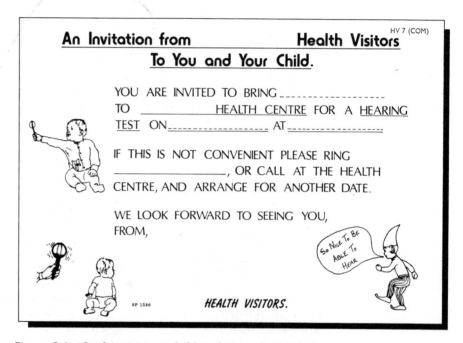

Figure 8.1 Card inviting a child to have a hearing test

By its very nature, there is a risk with screening of creating an uncomfortable relationship between the baby and the people close to it. Screening can also identify problems that do not actually exist—these are the 'false positives' that in screening for deafness greatly outnumber the 'true positives'. The effect can be to introduce a social construction of deafness (the understanding of a problem, the fear, the interference with personal identification) when there is no physical deafness.

3.6 Research

A feature of science is that all knowledge is always preliminary and open to negotiation. As a mode of understanding the world it can be contrasted with religious systems of knowledge which tend to provide complete answers. The amount that science leaves inadequately described is unsatisfying but it is not unreasonable to assume that it will extend its descriptions and explanations. It is always possible that more research will produce a better understanding of hearing, of the way that the auditory system sends signals distinguishing pitch to the brain, for example. While it is known that humans can usually hear a pure tone as high as 20,000 hertz, it is not clear how information is sent to the brain that can give the sensation of this pitch. The inner ear may be sufficiently sensitive to gather the information but the auditory nerve fibre is unable to send electrical impulses at anything like so high a rate to the brain. This lack of understanding about the link between the sensory apparatus of the ear and the brain is an area ripe for research. It is of course linked to the cochlear implant programme which is both limited by this lack of knowledge and yet may help by providing the opportunity to experiment with controlled stimulation of the auditory nerve.

This suggests that science may one day be able to understand and account for sensori-neural deafness—it may even be able to provide a technological aid to give a useful sort of hearing to people who would otherwise be deaf. But this time is always in the future; we are always being told that we have to invest resources now in research which will produce short-term benefit for a few, but potential future benefit for a great many more. This sort of issue is not about deafness as people experience it now but about the possibility that science will be able to change the nature of deafness. Nonetheless, there is a tendency to think in terms of the future and to imagine that science has something to say about deafness now.

3.7 Hearing aid technology

Science tends to operate at the level of the material and physical; persons, subjective accounts, feelings and wishes tend to be regarded as exterior to science. The scientific account is therefore much more at home with the technological solution to what has been perceived as a 'problem'. The need to review social features of knowledge that construct the problem can be put aside if there is a technical solution. With deafness there are two main technical solutions, both of which operate to limit or eradicate the physical manifestations of deafness. One that has already been mentioned is the cochlear implant which provides a direct sensory input to the inner ear. The other approach is amplification which involves adding a device that compensates for the sensory limitation of the person's hearing system. It depends on there being sufficient residual hearing.

◄ Activity 4

(a) Explore the ways in which hearing aids are sold. You should follow up advertisements and ask for information. Note how deafness is described and what claims are made for the efficacy of the hearing aid.

(b) You should ask a private firm for a hearing test. Make notes on the way hearing and deafness are discussed and described by the person who does the test. BE SURE TO RESIST BEING SOLD A HEARING AID WITHOUT SEEKING OTHER ADVICE. ◀

◀ Comment
Hearing aids are a commodity like transistor radios available to those who can afford to buy them. However, the medical connotations and the scientific basis of audiology become a resource in the promotion and selling of hearing aids. You may notice, and be impressed by, the use of jargon, references to technical efficiency and the techniques for measuring deafness. ◀

The hearing aid provides help to the hard of hearing, to those with a hearing loss and to some people who would otherwise be deaf. There has been great emphasis on the maximal use of residual hearing in the education of young children. What the account of the role of the hearing aid often does not include, however, are the inhibitions created by its presence, especially when it does not work for the user. You have already read the account by Lorraine Fletcher in Reader One about her discovery of her son's deafness. Her book goes on to describe how her son Ben was fitted for hearing aids before she understood what they might do for him. Getting impressions made for the hearing aids was itself a traumatic experience and the whole process raised expectations of what the aid might do. She describes the meeting later with the consultant to discuss the results of the audiological tests:

> He tells us that Ben's hearing can be boosted with hearing aids, 'but don't let anyone tell you that the kind of aid will make much difference because, quite honestly, it won't.' ... But we are still left with uncertainty. Will Ben hear or won't he? Is his loss over 100dB or under? What will he get through his aids? I actually ask this question. Again, the reluctance. 'He might get a sort of low rumble'. He might.
>
> (Fletcher, 1987)

Lorraine Fletcher describes how difficult it was to get Ben to wear the hearing aids supplied, how useless they seemed. And yet when the teacher for the deaf came, she started with the hearing aids. She advised that the ones he had were no good and she would get him a different type, but in the meantime they would work with the ones Ben had. Fletcher's account shows how there is a link between a medical diagnosis, the prescription of hearing aids and the educational methods for deaf children, based on speech. While both the consultant and the teacher for the deaf treated deafness as a remediable disability, they did not see it in quite the same way. The consultant did his best not to raise expectations about the level of hearing that would result from using a hearing aid and pointed out that the type of aid used made no difference. The teacher, on the other hand, changed the type of hearing aid.

One of the texts that caught Lorraine Fletcher's eye early on was a book entitled *Learning to Hear* (Whetnall and Fry, 1970):

> Now, this idea is completely new to me. We were told that Ben's deafness was permanent. I know that some physical handicaps can be alleviated by various kinds of training and therapy, but it has never

occurred to me that deafness might be curable in this way, and certainly none of the professionals we have spoken to has mentioned the possibility of Ben actually *learning* to hear. ... Ben falls asleep on the bus and I am able to skim through the book. In that short time I discover two new concepts: *auditory training* and *residual hearing*.

(Fletcher, 1987)

The hearing aid is necessary to maximize residual hearing and auditory training is necessary to teach the child to decode such sound signals as get through. Such an approach is dependent on the sound signals being at a sufficient level to decode—the fact that in Ben's case they were not at such a sufficient level took some time to become clear to his parents. The emphasis on hearing aids as a technical solution meant that less attention was paid to other approaches to helping Ben with the fact that he was deaf—in highlighting this, Lorraine Fletcher's book is really about recognizing the use of sign language as a communication system for a deaf child.

Lorraine and Ben Fletcher's experience is one in which hearing aids were a barrier to learning to be deaf. Another parent of a deaf child who has also written most powerfully of her experience is Kathy Robinson. Reader One also contains some extracts from her book which will have helped you to understand what it must be like to learn about the diagnosis of one's child as deaf. But her experience of education for her daughter Sarah was very different from the Fletchers' experience:

'I can hear better'

This advance, the most basic in the development of Sarah's hearing, had come about because I had had an ear mould made by the firm which supplied the radio-telemetry aids, instead of having one made through the National Health Service. Now I was able to turn the volume on her aid from its normal setting on '3' to its maximum setting on '9'—without it whistling!

I thought of the years when her hearing hadn't been fully utilized and I wanted to weep. Weep because of the sheer futility of it, and because it mattered. It mattered while her hearing was being trained. It mattered for her speech. Sarah had been wearing a hearing-aid worth hundreds and hundreds of pounds, and because of one worthless bit of plastic it hadn't even begun to touch her true hearing.

(Robinson, 1987a)

ITQ

What do think is the difference between the idea of 'Learning to be Deaf'— *social acceptance* (the title of the reading that began this unit and will have introduced this idea) and the idea of 'Learning to Hear' (the title of the book Lorraine Fletcher picked up)?

normality
overcomes disability
by technology

33

3.8 The power of science

Science is a powerful legitimator for ideas, concepts and definitions that enter into the broader social discourses. The scientific attitude underlies medicine and the development of technology but it is also a basis for discussing education and practical problems associated with deafness. It is as if science is disinterested, and yet, in that it is a way of understanding phenomena like deafness, it creates and sustains jobs for many people. Doctors and research scientists, audiologists and hearing aid technicians all have a vested interest in maintaining a particular way of understanding deafness.

There are two things to note about the effects of this scientific account of deafness. The first is that concern is with hearing and hearing loss rather than with deafness. We have seen that the scientific mode of understanding actually has very little to say about deafness as such. Nonetheless, it retains its powerful influence over the way other groups in society may see deafness by providing an authoritative general account of deafness in individuals. In this sense deafness is a residual category; it involves, largely, those people whom the scientific model cannot successfully describe as having a remediable hearing loss.

Secondly, the scientific model exerts an influence greater than it claims; people treat scientific sources as authoritative because of the general success of science in describing the material world. This tendency of us all to look to science, particularly in the form of medicine and technology, to describe and respond to a phenomenon such as deafness, ignores the limitations of science in this and many other areas. It also ignores the fact that deafness is not simply a material phenomenon—it is primarily about people and how they relate and communicate.

4 Deafness as deficiency

4.1 Deafness and cognition

Medicine and technology offer a view of deafness as the absence of hearing and present solutions in terms of the restoration of hearing. But this model of deficiency has been more influential than one that related only to medical matters and cure would have been. It pervades much of the discourse on deafness, particularly in areas of personality and intellectual development where the deaf person has been described in terms of deficit, of not being the same as hearing people and thus, by implication, inferior. An extreme statement of this position comes at the beginning of an article, entitled 'Linguistic Deficiency and Thinking' by Hans Furth published in 1971. He says:

> ... a number of new studies with deaf subjects have been reported. It seems that psychologists are beginning to realise the opportunity offered by the presence of linguistically deficient persons to test theories about the influence of language on various cognitive activities which are here subsumed under the word 'thinking'.

(Furth, 1971)

It seems ridiculous now to think about deaf people as being linguistically deficient in this way, but it is important to appreciate that if such a construction is made, or such a model imposed, it is difficult for certain research findings to be seen in any other way. A research study which takes certain proposals as given is likely to confirm those proposals. For example, the studies mentioned by Furth, based on a notion of linguistic deficiency, went on to ask questions about whether the lack of language affected certain intellectual abilities. If deaf people performed a task in the same way as hearing people, language was assumed to have no effect, but if they performed differently, language was seen as integral to the task. A typical study might be to investigate the role of language in formal logical thinking. The task would be non-verbal in the sense that the subjects would be given a problem in symbols and be expected to reply using symbols. For example, $\bar{H} \cdot \bar{B}$ means an object which is not a house ($\bar{H}$) and ($\cdot$) not blue ($\bar{B}$). The subject would then be presented with a picture of a yellow tree to which the answer would be 'true' expressed symbolically: that is, a yellow tree is not a house and not blue. Deaf subjects did less well than hearing subjects on this task and this was taken to mean that the task had a linguistic component (Furth and Youniss, 1965). In many other experiments deaf people did as well or better than hearing people, and then it was assumed that that particular task had no verbal component.

The experiments thus seemed to endorse the idea that deaf people were linguistically deficient without actually testing for this. There was no way a deaf person could behave which would lead the experimenter to question this basic assumption, which meant that, in effect, the experimental design itself did not allow the basic assumption to be questioned. The nature of scientific activity is such that the basic model is confirmed by the experiments until a paradigm shift takes place.

The idea of deaf people being linguistically deficient persisted until the late 1970s in psychological experiments and still persists in some writings about deafness. Lewis (1968), for example, suggested that deaf children's emotional development could be retarded by the lack of spoken language. While this view has now been discredited, it has been influential in a construction of deafness as deficiency and used to explain various intellectual and emotional variables, and this influence is still felt.

4.2 Deafness, personality and mental health

Unit 6 examined how these processes have operated in terms of personality and mental health. It exposed contradictions in the research findings and in the labelling system. It did not, however, include an examination of the deficiency model itself, as the emphasis of that unit; rather, what was considered important was an understanding of the processes by which some individuals are disabled within a society. However, because of its pervasiveness in much of the discourse about deaf people, and in particular in the discourse of professional groups who have the power to make decisions that concern deaf people, it is necessary to examine the deficiency model further.

◄ Reading
From Reader Two you should now read the following two articles:

Article 3.1, 'Cognition and Language' by Stephen Quigley and Peter Paul;

Article 3.2, 'Looking for Meaning in Sign Language Sentences' by Jim Kyle.

Do not worry too much about the content at this stage, but contrast the two approaches to study. ◄

Quigley and Paul look at questions of deficit and the influential work of Myklebust, though their conclusion is not proven. They suggest that earlier findings showing deaf people to be deficient on particular tasks were actually an indication of the inability of the experimenter to measure effectively. Kyle describes a study in which he tried to examine the way in which deaf people make sense of their world and shows how they coded stories differently but efficiently in terms of their ability to recall them.

4.3 Understanding difference or different understandings?

Now there may be differences between deaf and hearing people but it is the way in which we understand these differences that is critical. Let us take one particular example from Unit 5, in which the policy on integrating deaf children into mainstream schools was discussed. It was suggested that deaf children develop strategies to make it appear that they understand more than they actually do (Gregory and Bishop, in Article 5.11 in Reader Two). In most other accounts deaf children are considered to be failing because they are missing out on what is happening. This 'failure' is then seen as the fault of the individual child. An alternative view is that the mainstream school situation does not work for the deaf child because it does not provide adequate and consistent information. Seen from the deaf child's perspective, it could be argued that active and positive use is made of the information that *is* received. Several examples are given of the child responding with colour names to questions for which these were not the correct responses:

Teacher: … How can you skip?
Deaf child: White and brown.
…
Teacher: Do you know what vegetables he grows?
Deaf child: Pink.

(Gregory and Bishop, 1989)

But these children were not being stupid, they knew they were being asked questions and they knew that for many occasions a colour name would be appropriate and acceptable. The outcome of the responses may be more a reflection of teaching methods. Thus the alternative model is that deaf children are actively and positively making sense of their world through the information they get about it.

Let us now take another example. If deaf babies are observed with their hearing mothers their behaviour is often described as non-contingent, meaning that it does not follow on from what the mother is doing. Yet close analysis shows that the action of the child is understandable—the only difference being that what the child did was not what the mother expected. To take a common example: a hearing mother points to a doll's chair and says, 'Put the dolly on the chair'. The hearing child will most probably do this, but the deaf child is more likely to pick up the chair and look at it. The deaf child is not failing but is responding sensibly to the message received, which was that the chair is interesting to look at, to which the child makes a totally appropriate response. The only failure is that of the expectancy not matching the message.

The issue is the different ways in which difference is understood. Deaf people, in asserting a Deaf identity, are asserting difference. It is when a dominant group establishes norms and a minority group is constructed as deviant or deficient rather than different in the light of these norms, that problems arise.

5 Education

5.1 The deficiency model

In the last section we examined psychological discourse and saw how, in the past, it has constructed the notion of deaf people as deficient. Lack of hearing was associated with lack of language or deficient personalities. The notion of deafness as deficiency also pervades educational discourse. In Unit 5 it was pointed out that the very words chosen to describe the provision for deaf children—'services for the hearing impaired'—establishes this notion. The positive description 'deaf' is lost, and children are perceived as hearing children who are impaired. This is further reinforced by the emphasis laid on the measurement of hearing loss, and the categorization of children into different groups dependent on the degree of this loss.

◀ Reading
You have already looked at Article 5.1 by the British Association of Teachers of the Deaf in Reader Two which described the measurement of hearing loss, but you may wish to refresh your memory at this point. ◀

It is interesting to consider why there is this emphasis on these categories. It is not to do with the type of provision made: as was shown in Unit 5, the type of school attended was related more to the local authority in which a child lived, than to the degree of hearing loss attributed to the child. Neither does the category of loss define which educational approach is employed, except in the crudest way—this, too, is dependent on the philosophy of the education authority. The degree of loss has no general application, and these groupings are only applied within education. Deaf people themselves do not use them. Parents of deaf young people and deaf young people themselves rarely know how the loss has been defined, and questions on the extent of the deafness receive inconsistent replies.

Where the degree of hearing loss could possibly be relevant is in the prescription of hearing aids. However, this in itself would not appear to warrant the testing and re-testing of hearing that is a feature of education for deaf children. What it does is to reinforce the notion of deficiency—and all the more so because this deficiency can be classified and endorsed by scientific testing procedures. It puts the emphasis in education on trying to restore hearing rather than on evolving appropriate educational methods for use with deaf children.

5.2 The debate over communication methods

 ◀ Reading
You should re-read three articles on oralism, Total Communication and bilingualism in Reader Two. Rather than simply evaluating the approaches as you did in conjunction with Unit 5, this time note the goals of education implicit in each approach. The articles are:

5.5, 'A Critical Examination of Different Approaches to Communication in the Education of Deaf Children' by Wendy Lynas, Alan Huntington and Ivan Tucker;

5.6, 'Total Communication' by Lionel Evans;

5.7, 'Bilingualism and the Education of Deaf Children' by Miranda Llwellyn-Jones. ◀

Those advocating a strictly oral approach to education concentrate on the need for deaf children to be part of the hearing world:

> Oralists claim ... considerable optimism over the capability of even very deaf children to develop a fluency of spoken language which allows them to live comfortably and efficiently in hearing society. Oralists claim that the prospects have never been better for the very deaf child. As a result of recent advances—namely, the development of technologically sophisticated high powered hearing aids; an improved understanding of the process of language acquisition; more extensive parent guidance services and better educational practice—even very deaf children, that is those with profound hearing losses, can be enabled to produce and understand spoken language.
>
> ...
>
> ... oralists insist that educators have a *moral* responsibility to enable deaf children to acquire the *dominant* language of our society as a first priority. Only an oral approach allows the life objectives of the deaf person to be as wide as those of all other people.
>
> (Lynas *et al.*, 1988)

Being part of the Deef world is seen as second best or as a last resort:

> Oralists claim that deaf individuals without the ability to communicate
> orally are condemned to feel lonely and isolated in the hearing world.
> ... The deaf individual whose only significant social contacts are
> formed within the deaf group thus, arguably, leads a restricted life.
>
> ...
>
> We contend, however, that unless an oral–auditory approach is used in
> the education of deaf children, there is a serious risk that the deaf
> individual will have *no choice* but to form relationships of significance
> within the deaf-signing community. (Ibid.)

Moreover, there seems to be a fear of allowing children to use any form of
sign language:

> ... oralists maintain that a young deaf child, if persistently exposed to
> the visual communication of sign language will not learn to make best
> use of his *(sic)* residual hearing. Too much attention paid to visual
> input, it is argued, impedes the auditory development of deaf children
> and this may foreclose the possibility for some deaf children of ever
> achieving satisfactory levels of oral language and intelligible speech.
> (Ibid.)

You may remember how, in some accounts in Reader One, deaf people
described how they were forbidden to sign. They argued that children are
explicitly prevented from using one form of language, just because it is easy
and useful and they will come to depend upon it, and are encouraged to
develop another form of language which for some is difficult, and may even
be impossible.

Total Communication sets the same educational goals, in terms of spoken
and written English, but sees signing as appropriate to this in the form of
Sign Supported English. Bilingual approaches to education represent a shift
away from this to recognizing the significance of BSL and Deaf culture, and
to recognizing sign language as a legitimate language for education. In
Article 5.7 you read:

> Deaf children are more affected by negative attitudes than other
> minority groups as they are rarely brought up in an environment
> where their language is used by the rest of the community and family.
> Deaf people do not have the ethnic roots to fall back on and so have
> been even more at risk. Bilingualism fosters the link between sign
> language, deaf culture and the deaf community. The deaf are a
> handicapped group and also a linguistic minority, whose culture, and
> in a wider sense their whole way of life, is based on sign language.
> This is why sign language is of central importance when it comes to
> deaf people's equal participation, cultural identity and self respect.
> (Llwellyn-Jones, 1987)

Llwellyn-Jones goes on to say:

> Through sign language the deaf child gets knowledge and advice,
> learns values and standards, develops socially and emotionally, and
> learns how to express feelings. Through sign language, the cultural
> traditions of both deaf and hearing people can be brought to the deaf
> child. (Ibid.)

39

The differences in the approaches thus reflect not only controversy concerning the achievement of particular educational goals, but different perspectives on the educational process itself. The oralists state their educational objective as preparing deaf children for a hearing world and the discourse centres around ideas of 'normalization'. In Total Communication, the long-term objective would seem to be the same, but the approach is re-formulated to give recognition to the importance of signing. However, those advocating bilingualism write in terms of deaf children's cultural identity and self-respect.

It is, of course, the priority these different approaches give which is important and informs their respective constructions of deafness. The aims are not necessarily mutually exclusive. These different emphases, however, go some way to accounting for the seeming inadequacy of studies that have tried to compare different practices in the education of deaf children, for it is not simply a matter of different methods of education, but of different underlying ideologies.

5.3 Advising parents

Most parents of deaf children receive advice from the time their child is diagnosed from a peripatetic teacher of the deaf. Most welcome this, and most parents report that the advice and support they received was an important positive contribution.

While not wishing to undervalue the significance of the practice, we would like here to consider further the implications of advising parents.

ITQ

Without examining the content of the advice, what might be the implications of the existence of an advice service?

Firstly, and importantly, the existence of an advice service implies that there is real advice to be given; that is, that there is a correct way of doing things and that this is known by the teacher and not by the parent. This is an issue as much for teachers as it is for parents, as teachers do not see themselves as having answers. However, before the parent even meets the teacher, this is implicit within an advice-giving situation.

Moreover, if there is a correct way of doing things and the child is not seen to achieve the specified goals, then many parents will feel they have failed. Fortunately, this effect is not as strong now as it was in the 1970s when advice to parents clearly indicated that spoken language was a possibility for deaf children, and there was an implication that if the child did not learn to speak this constituted a failure on the part of the parents. A booklet entitled *You CAN Help Your Deaf Baby*, published by the National College of Teachers of the Deaf, that was frequently given to parents, said:

> Helping deaf children to understand what is said to them and to talk themselves is always a job that takes a lot of time. You need faith that

in the end many deaf children can talk and can become as normal as possible. They can certainly lead happy and useful lives … It's up to you. Will your deaf child fit into the world of hearing people, or will he (*sic*) grow up as a lonely person who can't understand and talk to other people? Of course he'll grow up to live a full and happy life, because you CAN help your deaf baby to talk.

(Williams, 1972)

So, if the child did not learn to speak, the failure, by implication, must lie with the parents.

The real issue here is the way in which deafness is constructed within the advice given. The conflicting advice about which methodology to use inevitably puts parents in a difficult position. In Unit 3, Section 9.5, you looked at the contrasting advice given to hearing parents of deaf children: on the one hand, advice advocating oral approaches, and on the other, advice advocating the use of sign language. Re-read this section now, looking at the implicit assumptions.

The advice given to parents differs not only in what it prescribes, but in its assumption about parental aspirations: 'Many parents tell us that what they want for their child is for him (*sic*) to fit into society, to be accepted socially; and paramount in their minds is that he should talk' (Nolan and Tucker, 1981), 'A comfortable social life should ordinarily involve the deaf person in the deaf community, and in whatever other circles he or she may choose' (Freeman *et al.*, 1981). Notice that, in the oral approach, fitting into society is equated with being able to talk, whereas the Total Communication approach assumes that the child, as an adult, will be part of the Deaf community.

5.4 The principle of normalization

An interesting feature of the advice of the oralists is the emphasis on normality—developing 'normal' language, being part of the 'normal' world. The idea of 'normality' has, superficially at least, positive connotations. What is normal seems to imply what is acceptable, and thus desirable. However, the concept of 'normality' is not straightforward. To start with, the word 'normal' has a number of meanings which are often confounded.

◀ Activity 5
You should look up the word 'normal' for yourself and consider the implications of the various meanings for its occurrence in the readings which form part of this section. ◀

If you have used the Chambers Shorter Dictionary, you will have been referred to the word 'norm', which means, among other things, 'the ordinary or most frequent state' and 'an acceptable standard of behaviour'. Thus there are two meanings with different emphasis: one with the focus on usual or frequent, and the other concerned with acceptability, which in turn implies that what is not acceptable is *ab*normal. Here lies a problem, for while writings about deafness that speak of the 'normal hearing world' may claim to use the term in the sense of most frequent or usual, they often carry with them the implication of a contrast with abnormal or unacceptable. It is the shift between these meanings which is problematic.

But there is another difficulty. 'Normal' is used to refer to aspects of human behaviour and development, which vary in the standards set for them. This is best illustrated by considering notions of language development. Those advocating oral approaches stress that they are advocating 'normal' language development, or 'normal standards of communication', 'It [the language development of the deaf child] follows a pattern very similar to the language development of normally hearing children' (Nolan and Tucker, 1981). But what is meant by 'normal' language and communication here? The oralists accept that the deaf child developing spoken language will be slower than his or her hearing contemporaries:

> We would anticipate that by the time he (*sic*) is three, you will have noted progress in his reception of speech and his own expression, which may by now contain some intelligible words, or may simply be becoming like the rhythmic babble of the normally hearing child at an earlier age.

> If you are the sort of person who likes to see immediate results for your work you could easily become disheartened by your child's lack of progress in speech and language in his earliest years... . Some children give back a great deal and others very little in the early years.
> (McCormick, 1976)

Yet in what sense is it normal not to have the capacity for communication until the age of three or five—not to be able to ask questions, or reflect on the day, or anticipate outings, Christmas etc.? Thus in this instance the use of the word 'normal' is highly selective, applying specifically to the use of spoken English and not to any 'normal' ability to communicate. Such advice also often contains the notion that parents should behave 'normally': 'Mother should be … stimulating him with a rich but normal language environment' and 'Hearing impaired children learn language naturally' (Nolan and Tucker, 1981).

Yet this, too, contains problems—for how does a hearing mother communicate with a 3-year-old child who does not speak? Does she talk about the child's activities as if he or she could understand, or does she adjust to the child's language level? A further problem in behaving 'normally' lies in the fact that deaf children, whether signing or speaking, will use the visual channel for communication. Instances of this are clear from the publication *A Parents Guide* by McCormick, first issued in 1976 but still available (although the National Deaf Children's Society, who used to send it out, have replaced it with a new pack for parents). This problem is implicitly recognized in the advice given in that publication. While much emphasis is placed on normal, natural behaviour, many elements are introduced which are not normal and natural:

> If I were to summarise the message contained within this series of articles in just a few words, I should say be natural with your child and notice how much of his behaviour is typical of a child of his age. The emphasis is therefore on normality, and your child's only privilege should be that of being exposed to a great deal more talking to than any child with normal hearing.

...

Nothing should be allowed to interfere with the normal parent child relationship. You will probably be more natural and successful with your child if you view him as a perfectly normal child whose only problem is that he cannot hear as well as you or I.

(McCormick, 1976)

Yet, despite all this stress on normality there are also several sections in the book describing how parents should behave in very specified non-normal ways:

It may be helpful to summarise briefly the conditions you should try to create if you are to give your hearing impaired child the best possible chance to make sense of the language he is exposed to, and which results from everyday activity and play experiences.

1 You should be at a reasonable distance from your child (three to four feet is ideal).

2 You face should be well illuminated and not in shadow.

3 The material being talked about should be brought up to the face so it is two to three inches from the lips. With larger objects you might have to angle yourself or the object so there is not too much distracting material in view at the same time. If the material is held even six inches away your child might focus on it so much visually that he misses the fine movements of your face as you speak.

4 You should speak clearly and naturally, in full phrases and sentences just as you do to any normally hearing child. The more enjoyment and interest you can secure from each opportunity for speech, the more your child will enjoy these situations and the greater will be the benefit he derives.

(Ibid.)

Thus, within a framework advocating explicitly normal behaviour, the parents are asked to behave in ways that cannot be normal.

Notions of normality are not just part of the language issue but are also included in discussions of integration, which is seen as providing a normal environment. Here again we have to unpack what is meant by 'normal'. Gregory and Bishop, in their article in Reader Two, show how presence in the 'normal' classroom is not equivalent to exposure to the 'normal' curriculum.

◀ Reading
You should now re-read Article 5.11, 'The Mainstreaming of Primary Age Deaf Children' by Susan Gregory and Juliet Bishop in Reader Two. ◀

This reading, as well as the points it makes about access to the curriculum, raises further issues in its discussions of the strategies children employed so that they appeared to understand. Teachers too colluded in these strategies, utilizing them in terms of their overall function in classroom management. However, there is something even more disturbing: appearing to be 'normal' seemed critical regardless of the way this was achieved. Lynas, in her book on integration, the conclusion to which is published in Reader Two, seems to see this as a laudable phenomenon:

> The research suggests, therefore, that if a deaf child has particularly pleasing qualities or special abilities his (*sic*) integration into a normal class will be facilitated. An implication of this finding is that those responsible for the education of deaf children should take every possible step to develop any talents or good personal qualities that the child may have.
>
> All the hearing impaired pupils and young people subscribed to the principle of normalisation in that they believed the major goal in deaf education should be teaching deaf children to talk. They believed that the ordinary school, in providing a normal spoken language environment, offered them as deaf pupils the best available means of acquiring the ability to talk normally. This view was held by deaf pupils and young people who used sign language together with those who eschewed any form of manual communication. Thus, virtually all the hearing impaired pupils and young people who had views on the matter stated a preference for education in the ordinary school.
>
> ...
>
> There seemed to be a universal desire among the deaf interviewees to acquire the behavioural norms of their normally hearing peers in order for them to be able to adapt to and be accepted in, a hearing speaking society. None of them questioned that they would need to conform to the expectations of the normally hearing if they were to cope with life as adults in a hearing speaking world.
>
> (Lynas, 1986)

◀ Reading
You should read again Article 5.9, 'Integrating the Handicapped into Ordinary Schools' by Wendy Lynas in Reader Two. This is the conclusion to the book from which the above quotations were taken.

You should then go on to re-read Article 5.10, 'Challenging Conceptions of Integration' by Tony Booth. This article discusses the notion of normalization from a different perspective. ◀

In educational terms, then, in the very provision of services to deaf children, to be deaf is to be deficient, to be not normal. The education system does not recognize the Deaf community, it sees no need to include deaf adults in the provision of education to deaf children. Teachers of the deaf are not expected to learn, and are often discouraged from learning, sign language—the language of Deaf people. You may wonder what this tells deaf children about what it is to be deaf.

6 Social policy

We have seen how medical discourse provides a context for confronting the physical presence of deafness, either at the moment that it is realized a child is born deaf or at the moment that the person's hearing declines such as to become a problem for them. Medicine can diagnose problems with hearing, remedying some and providing a basis for some technological intervention in many more cases. For many profoundly deaf people, however, there is very little that medicine or audiology can do. Their 'problems', then, are not to do with remedying their hearing deficiency but with living with deafness. We have seen how education and the acquisition of language are the next stage in the career of the deaf child: the way in which education and language use are presented to the deaf child helps to define what her or his deafness will mean. Education is always an important context for the establishment of an emerging personal identity, and the special nature of education for deaf children, with the enormous significance of communication, is equally as important in establishing their identity as deaf people.

A third stage in the deaf person's career is constructed by the discourse of social policy and welfare. The context this provides is linked to those of medicine and education since screening and special education are the products of social policies. But the state continues to accept a special responsibility towards deaf people once they are mature by making social work provision specially for deaf people.

6.1 Religious origins

Harlan Lane reminds us that Saint Paul said, 'Faith comes through hearing' and that Saint Augustine said of deafness, 'This impairment prevents faith' (Lane, 1984). The church seems to have regarded the deaf as lost souls who needed to be given its civilizing, institutional support and brought nearer to god. In writing about religion and the deaf, van Uden (1975) discusses what he sees as the difficulties faced by deaf people, who can neither hear nor speak, in attaining the 'authentic, selfless love' necessary for the Christian way of life. Van Uden's remarks are based on the belief that sign language is not adequate for teaching the subtlety of abstract thought: 'There is a special interaction of Christian religion and language. The reason is this: the Christian religion is a religion of revelation, which can be transmitted only with the aid of linguistic forms, although other more ... charismatic forms are not excluded' (van Uden, 1975).

Van Uden's views are based on the unsupported belief that spoken language is fuller and more capable than sign language of communicating abstract ideas and emotions, and it is not difficult to see how the practice of religion is focused on the spoken word. Prayer, even silent prayer, is a speech to god and the singing of hymns both praises god and creates a sense of unity amongst members of the church. For some religions, confession or giving testimony are important practices that gain some ritual significance from being spoken. All of these religious practices could be replicated using sign language or adapted to incorporate sign language users—but that would require the religious leaders to use sign language. This is exactly what happened in the mission movement in England when members of the clergy learnt sign language and used it to attend to Deaf peoples' spiritual and practical needs. George Firth has written a detailed history of the contribution of a number of individuals, many working through the church, to provide support of different kinds to members of the Deaf community. In telling the story of the Reverend Chris Griffiths, he mentions another link between religion and deafness. When asking an aunt why his parents were deaf she replied: 'Oh dear me, Christy my boy, your grandpa was a terrible blasphemer you know' (Firth, 1989).

The church has played its part in providing philosophical and institutional support to oralist education. But it must not be forgotten that secular views of the capacities of deaf people were not dissimilar from those of theologians. Lane mentions Condillac's belief that the deaf had no abstract ideas and no memory, and he cites Destutt de Tracy as asserting that the deaf, even after education, 'have a much more limited ability to think than we do' (de Tracy, quoted in Lane, 1984).

6.2 Missioners

Religion has influenced the way deafness is perceived and experienced in a much more active manner through the church missions established during the nineteenth century in the UK:

> The Churches, including the established Anglican Church, were influential in setting up societies for the Deaf with the specific task of 'preaching the Gospel to those who could not hear it for themselves'. The obvious problem of actually doing this to people who were stone deaf and largely illiterate was met by appointing 'Missionaries to the Deaf' or 'Missioners', who could speak to the Deaf by using 'Deaf sign language'.
>
> (Firth, 1989)

The aim of the missions was not merely to save souls but also to bring about changes in the lives of deaf people. As you will have learnt in Unit 7, the clergy involved in the missions not only learnt sign language but also developed skills that would enable them to help in educating and gaining employment for deaf people.

◄ Reading
You should re-read those sections of Articles 7.2 and 7.3 by George Taylor, and David Parratt and Brenda Tipping, respectively, in Reader Two, that refer to the role of the missions in establishing social services for deaf people. In what ways do you think the church and theology continue to be part of the process of socially constructing deafness? ◄

6.3 Legislation: empowerment or constraint?

You will already be aware of aspects of legislation from your reading of Units 5, 6 and 7; and the *Legislation Booklet* is a further useful resource for this section. In Unit 7 the role of legislation in establishing a social policy on deafness was discussed. Here we will look at how legislation also contributes to the construction of deafness by providing formal definitions. The importance of this is often in setting the boundaries on how state institutions, including the social services departments and education authorities, respond to deaf people and deaf children.

In the statute that founded the welfare state, the National Assistance Act, a category of disabled people was established which continues to be referred to in current legislation, including the 1986 Disabled Persons Act:

> A local authority shall have power to make arrangements for promoting the welfare of persons to whom this section applies, that is to say persons who are blind, deaf or dumb, and other persons who are substantially and permanently handicapped by illness, injury, or congenital deformity or such other disabilities as may be prescribed by the Minister.
>
> (National Assistance Act, 1948, Section 29)

The inclusion of deaf people in such a broad category of disabled people is not popular amongst many in the Deaf community. The effect is that deaf people are entitled to be assessed for services under the Acts which relate to disabled people. Under the National Assistance Act these included giving people instruction in their own homes on how to overcome the effects of their disabilities, and providing workshops, hostels and recreational facilities (Section 29 (4)). The Act also provided for registers to be kept of those people for whom provision was made under Section 29.

The major piece of legislation affecting services is the Chronically Sick and Disabled Persons Act of 1970. This extended the responsibility of local authorities to provide services in the home for disabled people—including adaptations to 'secure the greater safety, comfort or convenience' of disabled people. Section 2 also included clauses requiring the local authority to 'facilitate the taking of holidays', 'provision of meals for the person whether in his home or elsewhere' and 'the provision of for that person, or assistance to that person in obtaining, a telephone and any special equipment necessary to enable him to use a telephone' (Chronically Sick and Disabled Persons Act, 1970, Section 2 (1)(h)).

This sort of legislation is not appropriate for many deaf people—they are not disabled in the sense of needing help in the home although they may need equipment (such as a doorbell lamp) that can be provided through the local authority. Most of the Chronically Sick and Disabled Persons Act is directed at people with mobility problems and later sections are specifically concerned with access to buildings, provision of appropriate toilets, the use of invalid carriages and disabled persons' badges for cars. There is considerable variation in the provision of facilities by local authorities under this Act.

What is noticeably absent from the legislation is any provision for deaf people as a linguistic or communicatively disadvantaged group. There are no provisions, for example, requiring the availability of translating services into sign language. As Taylor points out, 'the criteria of need are determined by authorities in the light of available resources, not the needs of the disabled themselves' (Taylor, 1986a). Indeed, a major problem with interpreting the legislation relating to disabled people is the lack of guidance on what is meant by disability and the room for widely varying interpretations by different local authorities.

Under the Education Act 1981, deaf children are also treated as disabled and defined through having a 'learning difficulty'. A child will count as having learning difficulties if:

> (b) he has a disability which either prevents or hinders him from making use of educational facilities of a kind generally provided in schools, within the area of the local authority concerned, for children of his age; or
>
> (c) he is under the age of five years and is, or would be if special educational provision were not made for him, likely to fall within paragraph (a) or (b) when over that age.
>
> (Education Act 1981, Section 1)

The main substance of the Act is to direct education authorities to provide special education within ordinary schools provided that the child is 'receiving the special education he requires'. This does not include specifying how communication difficulties shall be dealt with and indeed a later clause in this section specifically excludes learning difficulties to do with language:

> A child is not to be taken as having a learning difficulty solely because the language (or form of the language) in which he is, or will be, taught is different from a language (or form of a language) which has at any time been spoken in his home.
>
> (Education Act 1981, Section 1 (4))

It seems most unlikely that the use of sign language was considered in the drafting of this section. However, the effect is that a child who is disabled through 'hearing loss' is entitled to special educational provision whereas the child who communicates in a different language such as British Sign Language is not.

Thus legislation defines deaf people as certain sorts of persons with certain sorts of needs. In this sense what it is to be deaf is constructed by society through its laws and regulations. Institutions acting on behalf of society also construct the situation of deaf people but in less visible ways. As we have seen with medicine and education, knowledge about deafness is applied by professional staff working through organizations (the health service, the school system). These organizations and professions have responsibilities extending beyond deafness that affect the way they deal with deaf people.

7 Language, knowledge and power

An issue that should be emerging for you now that you are this far into the course, is that language is of central importance in establishing who we are as individuals. This includes making distinctions between people, such as that made between hearing and deaf people. Language is not only the process by which such categories of people are defined, it is also the mode of human practice which puts the categories into operation and makes the distinctions real in the lives and relationships of people. It is this recognition of the centrality of language in shaping social life that is the basis for the account by Berger and Luckmann of the 'social construction of reality':

> Language originates in and has its primary reference to everyday life; it refers above all to the reality I experience in wide-awake consciousness, which is dominated by the pragmatic motive (that is, the cluster of meanings directly pertaining to present or future actions) and which I share with others in a taken-for-granted manner.
>
> (Berger and Luckmann, 1967)

In Unit 3 you looked at the way in which language constructs experience and, in particular, at the way in which different languages partition the world in different ways or differ in the way in which they specify aspects of the world. A view from within linguistics that supports the role given to language by Berger and Luckmann is that offered by the Sapir/Whorf hypothesis which asserts that the particular language someone uses directly affects and shapes that person's view of the world. Whorf was a student of Sapir and his study of the Hopi Indians contributed significantly to this view of the power of language. Of particular interest was the Hopi concept of time. The Hopi language: '... is seen to contain no words, grammatical forms or expressions that refer directly to what we call 'time' or to past, present or future ...' (Whorf, 1956).

Whorf argues that the structure of the Hopi language actually means that time is different for them. He observes that the Hopi have:

> ... no general notion or intuition of time as a smooth flowing continuum in which everything in the universe proceeds at an equal rate, out of a future, through a present, into a past; or in which, to reverse the picture, the observer is being carried in the stream of duration continually away from a past and into a future.
>
> (Whorf, 1956)

There are problems with this analysis but it is nonetheless interesting to apply it to BSL. Do Deaf people for whom BSL is their main language think differently about time? Perhaps Deaf people who are bilingual could attempt an answer to such a question. As you learnt in Unit 3, BSL represents time spatially and establishes the process of time in a specific relation to the body. The future is in front of the person, the past is behind them. The signs for after and ahead, for example, are established by a changing spatial relationship between the two hands. In spoken and written English concepts of both time and space are usually carried by separate and abstract notions—although English speakers do talk of the future as being in front, and of a 'long' time and 'long' things.

7.1 Social construction

The concept of 'social construction' sounds odd when applied to something like deafness; deafness is so obviously physical, a bodily impairment. But deafness is framed by the social context in which it occurs. It is the particular way in which society understands and responds to deafness that determines exactly what deafness means, how the deaf person is treated and what he or she faces. For example, deafness may be construed as a problem that is visited on the individual and to which society must respond. However, communities could construe deafness in such a way that the deaf person is not seen as impaired and does not experience his or her deafness as a handicap. In the account by Nora Groce (1985), of deafness over three centuries on Martha's Vineyard, deafness seems to be no more an impairment or a handicap than having red hair.[2] The fascination of Groce's account lies in how differently deafness was construed by that society from the way it is by our own.

The suggestion that ideas are not 'pure' but are 'socially constructed' is not, of course, new. It can be traced back to Francis Bacon's early seventeenth century account of the 'idols of the mind'—different features of human social life that affected and distorted perception (Bacon, 1985). In modern times the sociology of knowledge has proposed that the ideas that constitute knowledge do not originate exclusively in a real world that pre-exists human knowledge of it. Instead, ideas are either wholly or in part 'socially determined' (Mannheim, 1936) or 'socially constructed' (Berger and Luckmann, 1967). In Section 3 we saw how a social construction account of knowledge has developed in sociological analyses of science and medicine. The notion of the social determination or social construction of knowledge has frightening consequences because it undermines our sense of how we experience the world.

7.2 The naturalistic and social perspectives of knowledge

When we see a bird fly, we take it that our knowledge is of the bird, it is determined by what the bird is. This is a 'natural determination' account in which we presume that it is our intelligence applied to the information from our senses that leads to our knowledge of the bird. We can describe it to demonstrate our knowledge. Probably we can name it (a swallow) and describe features of it (a forked tail). We know that as a bird, it flies; that is, it moves through the air by beating its wings. The action of its wings on the substance of the air enables the bird both to defeat the force of gravity that is pulling it to the ground, and to move forward. But how do we know all this? Our senses, our eyes, may apply the knowledge to this particular bird but it is not our eyes that originate the concept of 'swallow' or the mechanics of flight.

Of course, someone told us. A swallow was pointed out and named by someone else (a parent, a teacher, a friend, even a book) and the distinguishing features were noted (the style of flight, the call, that

[2] You will have already read the extract of Groce's account—which is included as Article 1.2 in Reader Two—in conjunction with your study of earlier units in the course.

'unmistakable' tail). So, the knowledge that individual people have actually has a social origin. We learn about the world not from the world but from other humans. As people, our knowledge is not simply determined by 'nature', it is determined by what we are taught or what is made available for us to learn.

But the naturalistic perspective will insist that the social context does not determine the knowledge, it is merely the means by which knowledge is passed on. The natural determination thesis will claim that, originally, the knowledge was derived from the natural world, that the humans who generated the knowledge (which was subsequently passed on socially) actually studied the bird, observing it, distinguishing it from other birds, noting its features, distilling a description of birds and eventually of this particular type of bird. The information that lies at the heart of the knowledge is derived directly from nature.

We can see that there are two realms, presumed in this debate to be separate: the natural and the social. The natural is a reality out there, that exists independently of humans and whatever they do. The swallow would fly past whether it was noticed or not, it would be the same sort of thing with the same characteristics and capabilities whether or not it was named or studied or its abilities were understood by human beings. The other realm, the social, is the process of human interaction and collaboration in which experience is shared and stored through communication. Experience itself is solitary but we are able to share experience in a reflective mode by telling each other what we experience. We can also co-experience (both look at the bird at the same time) so that when we come to share the experience we may confirm what we thought went on ('Did you see that swallow?', 'Yes!').

There is no end to the debate between a naturalistic perspective and a social one. It is difficult to deny the existence of the natural world because it is so present to our experience, so much a part of our everyday life. But on the other hand, the more one questions the 'natural attitude' the more one finds that there is a social dimension to what is going on in our understanding of the world. The tools with which the world is reduced to knowledge are essentially linguistic. Even mathematics, which enables a precise and unequivocal description of phenomena, is a system of signs used to represent the world, to stand for it in communication. It is a form of language and, although pure in itself (i.e. systematic and unequivocal), it is always wrapped in spoken or written language that puts it in context and provides the link between systematic knowledge (perhaps an account in a book, of the mechanics of a swallow's flight) and the direct experience of watching the swallow fly.

The example of watching a bird fly may seem some way from considering what deafness is. But what is meant by the term 'deafness' comes to us as knowledge in much the same way as our knowledge of birds. There are both elements of a 'natural perspective' and features of 'social construction' that contribute to what we understand by deafness.

7.3 What does 'deafness' mean?

There are a number of ways in which deafness is defined in different social contexts. We have seen that a scientific model is dominant in both medicine and the technological response to limits to hearing. There are various formal 'discourses' in which experts speak and write, in English, about deafness. We have glimpsed how medicine (Section 3), education (Section 5) and social policy (Section 6 and Unit 7) construe what deafness is within their formal discourses. The formality of these accounts derives from a number of features. The accounts are written down, which makes them fixed, and reference can be made back to them at different points in time. The same accounts as written texts can be read by many different people at the same or a different time, in the same or different places. What is more, the accounts are legitimated in a number of ways. Simply transforming the text into print, putting it between covers—publishing it—means that someone who knows what will be read has approved of it. The authors often have formal qualifications that enable them to speak with authority from within a particular formal discourse. Styles of writing make reference to research or previous authoritative opinion in order to support what is being said and to link texts, weaving them into a discourse with themes and continuities.

In the realm of medicine, what deafness means is based on the limits or lack of a capacity in the person's body to respond to the sounds around them, especially the sound of the spoken word. Within medicine deafness is defined in two ways, both having a scientific and systematic basis. First, deafness as deficiency of hearing is defined by audiology, by measuring what volume and frequency of sound can be heard. Second, deafness is defined by its cause, expressed in terms of the anatomical site of the deficiency. The discourse of medicine defines deafness as a material form, the absence (or relative absence) of hearing. This deficiency model of deafness (Section 4) can be contrasted with the views of deafness you read about in the Introduction when you were referred to the article by Padden and Humphries in Reader Two.

The medical discourse is linked to a technological discourse which articulates how the material absence of hearing can be remedied by prosthesis. The medical discourse is also linked to that of education which offers a non-material remedy of 'learning to hear'. Here, though, the discourse of education defines deafness in terms of human development, the ability to learn the spoken form of language. In educational terms the deficiency of deafness lies in the lack of social capacities of speech communication and ability to learn through speech, the principal channel of communication for learning. There are links with the medical and technological discourses because the diagnosis of deafness and its degree originate with medicine, and the remedial effect of hearing aids is treated as a prior necessity.

The discourse of social policy again responds to social deficiencies but this time deafness is defined in terms of competence to live independently. The discourse addresses the ability of the person to deal with the practical aspects of life, securing employment, housing, a social life. Deafness is defined as a form of inability to cope, a handicap which disables the person. This does not mean that all deaf people are defined similarly but that deafness is a sufficient basis for requiring material support, personal advice or specialist equipment.

There are other discourses that define deafness which we have not dealt with so thoroughly. There is in particular the religious discourse within which the spiritual deficiency of the deaf person was raised. The religious desire to save souls meant that there was a serious attempt to 'enlighten' the deaf through an education that would enable them to understand the word of god (see van Uden, 1975). This religious definition of the presumed lack of capacity of deaf people to reason without first achieving competence as speakers of English has clearly influenced the tradition of educating deaf children. It has also no doubt had a part to play in the classification and treatment of deafness within psychiatry. The religious definition has also played a major role in the development of a social policy towards deaf people.

Another discourse on which we have only briefly touched is that of the 'charities', the non-state sector organizations that focus attention on the needs of deaf people. Some of these organizations have their origins in a religious imperative to provide charity to those defined as needy. The largely secular discourse of the modern charities has perhaps more in common with the definitions of deafness that are generated within the discourse of social policy.

This course is, you should be saying by now, just the same—another discursive construction like those we have been describing.

ITQ

While the above statement is true, it is also quite unavoidable and quite appropriate—ask yourself why you have read this far through the course. Do you feel that this course has developed a range of perspectives and avoided treating one account of deafness as authoritative to the exclusion of all others?

7.4 Social integration

That deaf people should be integrated into 'normal' society is often the aim of strategies which deal with deafness as a problem. These strategies are usually sponsored by the state (although in the past the church played a dominant role) on behalf of society as a whole. One of the consequences of this is that the social interests of hearing society and deaf people are presumed to be the same. The ideal is for deaf people to be as 'normal' as possible; that is, to be able to function independently on the same terms as other members of society. The notion of 'normality' underlies the move from individual experience to shared experience and to the shared understanding of meanings. In so far as actions are based on what is taken to be normal these become social norms; in this way beliefs about what is 'normal' lead to determine individual actions and social responses. In Section 5.4 of this unit you will have seen how the concept of 'normality' has provided a guiding principle in offering education that will integrate deaf children into hearing society.

The integration of groups such as deaf people into wider society serves the needs of the whole society by minimizing division. The fewer separate groups the less potential there is seen to be for conflict. The integrationist approach seeks to maximize the ability of deaf people to communicate with hearing people. This, it should be noted, does not involve a reciprocal effort by hearing people to communicate with deaf people in their language. Deaf people remain disadvantaged when compared to hearing people in a wider society that is organized around the ability to hear.

The social identity of individual deaf people is determined partly by their experience and partly by the social categories which define deafness in the contexts in which they find themselves. A deaf person's identity is not only determined by their own experience of deafness but also by how hearing friends and work colleagues respond to them, how much and what sort of contact they have with other deaf people, what images of deaf people they find in the wider culture, that frame their own experience.

But some Deaf people feel that their interests are not the same as those of the rest of society. Their deafness means that they have a particular mode of communication, sign language, that would be jeopardized by complete integration. They see their interests as individuals in sustaining and supporting their own sense of identity as Deaf people, not as people who are striving to live up to the norm of being hearing. As a group of Deaf people their interests may be better served by establishing a Deaf sub-culture which mediates links between Deaf people and the wider society. The effect is to establish a strong cultural basis for the identity of Deaf people within their own community and provide a support network and a good basis for negotiating with the wider hearing society.

7.5 Language and power

There are three ways in which this course has focused on language as important to the social construction of deafness. First, it is through language that our experience of the world is structured and the meaning of deafness is constructed. This means that the world and culture experienced by someone whose first language is BSL will be somewhat different from that experienced by someone whose first language is English. This leads to the possibility of distinguishing a Deaf community as a cultural milieu within the wider society. It also leads to the second focus on language, the exclusion and denial of sign language which constitutes a linguistic and cultural oppression of Deaf people. Spoken English is treated as the dominant language and sign language as, at best, a poor imitation of it and, at worst, a crude series of pre-linguistic gestures.

Third, it is through language that discourses such as those of medicine, education and social policy are constructed. These in turn exert power over those people marked out by the categorial distinctions the discourses make. The power is actually exercised by those people who act as agents of society (doctors, teachers, social workers), but the rules and values which determine their actions derive from the discourse which provides the context for their practice.

7.6 Knowledge and power

In this third focus on the role of language in the social construction of deafness, there is a conjunction of language, knowledge and power that underlies both of the other foci and is indeed at the heart of the process of social construction. Michel Foucault's work has explored how power operates both within discourse to give it its particular form and outside discourse to affect the lives people live. In the 'Orders of Discourse' (1971), for example, he describes the process of excluding contributions that do not comply with particular forms (such as using the right jargon or being published in the right way). He describes the divisions between different types of knowledge and the 'fellowship of discourse' which sustains these by defining a limited set of participants through both formal and informal means. It is these qualified participants, of course, who manage and enforce the rules of exclusion and division.

Just as power operates within discourse to determine what counts as knowledge, so knowledge as power operates to legitimate particular human practices which constrain the bodies and activities of people. Foucault has shown how various discourses are used as a legitimating context for control—for example, the discourse of reason and unreason for controlling the mad (Foucault, 1967), and that of restraint and surveillance for controlling prisoners and workers (Foucault, 1977). It is important to stress that there is no suggestion that knowledge is used cynically in these contexts or that there is a conspiratorial intention to exploit the mad or the imprisoned. What is going on is that the discourse gives a structured response to categories of people who are seen as not the same as everyone else. The discourse addresses and defines the difference, and generates a coherent response in the form of controlling practices. What Foucault shows is that the definition and response are not independent of other, seemingly separate, social processes. The definition and treatment of the mad are tied up with the emergence of philosophical reason and beliefs about the link between reason and certain ordered ways of living. The modern treatment of prisoners is based on the principle that if people are watched, if their transgressions are seen by another, they will be subject to control without force. The treatment of prisoners is linked to an understanding about the way of governing, of exercising control over a populace and of the nature of human beings.

The discourse of medicine, with its claim to legitimacy through science, has had enormous influence over the lives of deaf people. It has defined their deafness, marked them as deaf individuals in a hearing society. In doing so it has directed them towards other practices that have in their turn been influenced by medical discourse—in particular, education and social policy. The content of these three perspectives on deafness has defined both how deaf people see themselves and how they are set in a particular relationship to a society which uses spoken English as its principal mode of communication. What we hope to have shown is that the discursive process by which knowledge about deafness is generated, involves social practices which are already embedded with ideas that affect how deafness will be seen; that is, deafness as a physical deficiency, and normality as participation in a society dependent on using spoken English.

7.7 The social reconstruction of deafness

The social construction of reality in general and of deafness in particular is a continuous process. It is a social process and one in which everyone takes part whether they like it or not. It is, however, a process in which power, interest and enthusiasm affect outcomes; those who wish to see changes brought about have a number of things they can do to construct deafness in the way they want to see it. We have argued that the social construction of deafness has occurred through a number of discourses—medicine, popular culture, education, social policy—all dominated by a hearing perspective. But a Deaf perspective is emerging that is reconstructing what deafness means by focusing on the experience of Deaf people.

Unravelling history, questioning existing histories and reinterpreting what has been written are ways of beginning to bring about change in the social construction of deafness. Harlan Lane (1984), by claiming that Deaf people are angry and giving them good reasons why they should be angry, will help to make them angry. He has intervened very successfully in a process of rewriting the history of deafness from the perspective of deaf people. He is not writing the history of services for the deaf or of education for the deaf but claims he is writing the history of Deaf people. Padden and Humphries (1988) have presented the accounts of Deaf people themselves, partly to write the unwritten history of the experience of being Deaf in a hearing society, and also to provide a valuable reference point for contemporary experience of deafness.

The fact that the Deaf community expresses itself in a language that does not have a written form means that it is more difficult for Deaf people's accounts to be formalized in the way that the hearing accounts of deafness from doctors, teachers, social workers and even parents of deaf children have been. For some Deaf people, to write might mean translating what they wish to say from sign language into written English. Yet this often involves losing some of the quality of what was present in sign, and may under-represent the power of the communication because what is left in English sounds awkward or simplified. It is for this reason that so much of what is written about deafness, even by those who wish to stress the importance of Deaf language and culture, is written by hearing people.

Nonetheless, there are some accounts of deafness by Deaf people—there are a number in Reader One. And Deaf people have been expressing themselves and their feelings about living in a hearing society for some time. The hearing society seems to find it hard to hear what they say—Deaf commentators do not sound so authoritative. Indeed, they may sound very difficult to understand to the hasty hearing person. Deaf people are less likely to have succeeded in the hearing world sufficiently to have a position of status which will enable them to attract the interest of a publisher, and they are less likely to have achieved sufficient educational status to claim authority from within an academic discipline.

Establishing a Deaf culture can involve 'raising the consciousness' of Deaf people as a group with group interests. These can be expressed as demands about how Deaf people should be treated and what services they expect. The Charter of Rights of the Deaf includes a set of demands about the rights of the deaf child to be treated '... first and foremost as a person whose talents for knowledge of languages and for receiving education is unimpaired by his or her deafness' (National Union of the Deaf, 1982).

The demands also require that the child be allowed to communicate in a method which he or she prefers, that teachers possess proficiency in the use of Total Communication, and that the child has the right to refuse to wear hearing aids. The list of proposed rights is interesting because it puts decision making primarily in the hands of the child, not in the hands of the parents. It also bases its demands on the recognition of the Deaf child's different language and culture—this is to be reflected in literature, television and the media, and access to equal opportunities and participation is to be facilitated by the spread of British Sign Language and the use of interpreters.

In articulating demands as a unified group, Deaf people are beginning to reconstruct what deafness means, based not on the authoritative accounts of professionals and academics but on the experiences of Deaf people themselves. The National Union of the Deaf (NUD) speaks with a clearly deaf voice in a way that other deaf pressure groups do not. The NUD is not afraid, for example, to accuse the English education system of genocide through the repression of sign language and Deaf culture in a predominantly oralist system. The conflict between a construction by hearing people of deafness as a hearing deficiency and by Deaf people as a culture based on the predominant use of sign language, is potentially bitter and extreme. But not all deaf experiences are the same and even those who have experienced an inflexible and unenlightening education system may not feel that an aggressive assertion of Deaf culture is going to be successful. Some deaf people, especially those with some residual hearing, are able to integrate 'normally' in a hearing community—they do not wish to identify with a different, Deaf community.

There are compound problems in maintaining the continuous identity of a Deaf culture. First, deafness does not tend to run in families so that there is usually a cultural tension between the generations of families with deaf members. Second, the incidence of deafness means that there are not a large number of deaf people in one place. The exceptions are schools for deaf children where there is potential for building a Deaf community that will be difficult to maintain, especially in less populated parts of the country. Integrated education has reduced the number of such schools and restricted their role in Deaf culture.

In establishing their identity as a group, Deaf people are claiming a cultural identity which can be seen as a sub-culture of the main culture. Dual membership is quite possible; in relating to family and friends one can 'integrate' and in relating to deaf people one can be 'deaf'. There may be conflicts between the two social group identities but people everywhere share cultural identifications with sub-groups.

◀ Activity 6
In Unit 9, you will begin to learn more about the response of the Deaf community to the social construction of deafness. Before looking at that material, sketch out some strategies that you think might help to change the way deafness is seen in society. How can the processes of social construction be influenced? ◀

Suggestions for further reading

If you are interested in the ways in which a history of the Deaf community is being reconstructed in the UK, you might like to have a look at the following two books:

GRANT, B. (1990) *The Deaf Advance: The History of the British Deaf Association*, East Lothian, The Pentland Press.
In *The Deaf Advance*, the history of the British Deaf Association is told.

JACKSON, P. (1990) *Britain's Deaf Heritage*, East Lothian, The Pentland Press.
This book tells the history of deaf people in Britain over the past 300 years, with particular attention paid to education and to the growth of the Deaf community.

Both these books have been published to celebrate the centenary (in 1990) of the British Deaf Association.

If you would like to read more about 'social construction', you may find the following of interest, though none of them discusses the social construction of *deafness*:

BERGER, P. and LUCKMAN, T. (1967) *The Social Construction of Reality*, Harmondsworth, Penguin Books.
This is a classical and seminal work on this topic, which has had a major influence in the area.

WRIGHT, P. and TREACHER, A. (eds) (1982) *The Problem of Medical Knowledge: Examining the Social Construction of Medicine*, Edinburgh, Edinburgh University Press.
This book gives a social constructionist account of medicine and medical knowledge.

GERGEN, K. and SHOTTER, J. (eds) (1989) *Texts of Identity*, London, Sage Publications.
A recent book, illustrating the application of ideas and social construction to a variety of topics.

References

BACON, F. (1985) *The Essays*, John Pitcher (ed.), Harmondsworth, Penguin Books.

BALLANTYNE, J. and MARTIN, J. (1984) *Deafness*, 4th edn, London, Churchill Livingstone.

BERGER, P.L. and LUCKMANN, T. (1967) *The Social Construction of Reality*, Harmondsworth, Penguin Books.

BOOTH, T. (1988) 'Challenging conceptions of integration', in Gregory, S. and Hartley, G.M. (eds) (1990) *Constructing Deafness*, London, Pinter Publishers. (D251 Reader Two, Article 5.10)

BRIEN, D. (1981) 'Is there a deaf culture?', in Gregory, S. and Hartley, G.M. (eds) (1990) *Constructing Deafness*, London, Pinter Publishers. (D251 Reader Two, Article 2.5)

BRITISH ASSOCIATION OF TEACHERS OF THE DEAF (1985) 'Audiological descriptors', in Gregory, S. and Hartley, G.M. (eds) (1990) *Constructing Deafness*, London, Pinter Publishers. (D251 Reader Two, Article 5.1)

BROWNING, G.G. (1986) *Clinical Otology and Audiology*, London, Butterworth.

DAVIS, H. (1978) 'Abnormal hearing and deafness', in Davis, H. and Silverman, S.R. (eds) *Hearing and Deafness*, 4th edn, New York, Holt, Reinhart and Winston.

EVANS, L. (1982) 'Total communication', in Gregory, S. and Hartley, G.M. (eds) (1990) *Constructing Deafness*, London, Pinter Publishers. (D251 Reader Two, Article 5.6)

FIRTH, G. (1989) *Chosen Vessels: A Tribute to Those Pioneers in the Care of the Deaf*, Sydney Rd, Exeter, G.C. Firth.

FLETCHER, L. (1987) *Language for Ben: A Deaf Child's Right to Sign*, London, Souvenir Press.

FLETCHER, L. (1990) 'Discovery and diagnosis', in Taylor, G. and Bishop, J. (eds) (1990) *Being Deaf: The Experience of Deafness*, London, Pinter Publishers. (D251 Reader One, Article 3)

FOUCAULT, M. (1967) *Madness and Civilization; A History of Insanity in the Age of Reason*, London, Tavistock.

FOUCAULT, M. (1971) 'Orders of discourse', inaugural lecture delivered at the College de France, *Social Science Information*, vol. 10 (2), pp. 7–30.

FOUCAULT, M. (1977) *Discipline and Punish; The Birth of the Prison*, Harmondsworth, Penguin Books.

FREELAND, A. (1989) *Deafness: The Facts*, Oxford, Oxford University Press.

FREEMAN, R.D., CARBIN, C.F. and BOESE, R.J. (1981) *Can't Your Child Hear?*, London, Croom Helm.

FURTH, H.G. (1971) 'Linguistic deficiency and thinking: research with deaf subjects 1965–69', *Psychological Bulletin*, no. 1, pp. 58–72.

FURTH, H.G. and YOUNISS, J. (1965) 'The influence of language and experience in the discourses and use of logical symbols', *British Journal of Psychology*, vol. 56 (4), pp. 381–90.

GRANT, B. (1990) *The Deaf Advance: The History of the British Deaf Association*, East Lothian, The Pentland Press.

GREGORY, S. (1976) *The Deaf Child and His Family*, London, George Allen and Unwin.

GREGORY, S. (1990) 'Deafness in fiction', in Gregory, S. and Hartley, G.M. (eds) (1990) *Constructing Deafness*, London, Pinter Publishers. (D251 Reader Two, Article 8.1)

GREGORY, S. and BISHOP, J. (1989) 'The mainstreaming of primary age deaf children', in Gregory, S. and Hartley, G.M. (eds) (1990) *Constructing Deafness*, London, Pinter Publishers. (D251 Reader Two, Article 5.11)

GROCE, N. (1985) 'Everyone here spoke sign language', in Gregory, S. and Hartley, G.M. (eds) (1990) *Constructing Deafness*, London, Pinter Publishers. (D251 Reader Two, Article 1.2)

HIGGINS, P. (1980) 'Outsiders in a hearing world', in Gregory, S. and Hartley, G.M. (eds) (1990) *Constructing Deafness*, London, Pinter Publishers. (D251 Reader Two, Article 2.1)

JACKSON, P. (1990) *Britain's Deaf Heritage*, East Lothian, The Pentland Press.

JEFFREYS, S. (1989) 'Does it matter if they did it?', in Lesbian History Group (eds) *Not a Passing Phase,* London, Pluto Press.

KANNAPELL, B. (1982) 'Inside the deaf community', *Deaf American*, vol. 34 (4).

KELLER, H. (1913) 'How I became a socialist', in *Out of the Dark* (collection of essays), New York, Doubleday.

KELLER, H. (1968) *Midstream: My Later Life*, New York, Greenwood. (First published 1929.)

KLOBAS, L.E. (1988) *Disability Drama in Television and Film*, London, McFarland.

KYLE, J. (1983) 'Looking for meaning in sign language sentences', in Gregory, S. and Hartley, G.M. (eds) (1990) *Constructing Deafness*, London, Pinter Publishers. (D251 Reader Two, Article 3.2)

KYLE, J. and WOLL, B. (1985) *Sign Language: The Study of Deaf People and Their Language*, Cambridge, Cambridge University Press. (D251 Set Book)

LADD, P. (1988) 'The modern deaf community', in Gregory, S. and Hartley, G.M. (eds) (1990) *Constructing Deafness*, London, Pinter Publishers. (D251 Reader Two, Article 2.3)

LANE, H. (1984) *When The Mind Hears: A History Of The Deaf*, London, Penguin Books.

LAWSON, L. (1981) 'The role of sign in the structure of the deaf community', in Gregory, S. and Hartley, G.M. (eds) (1990) *Constructing Deafness*, London, Pinter Publishers. (D251 Reader Two, Article 2.2)

LESBIAN HISTORY GROUP (1989) 'Introduction' in Lesbian History Group (eds) *Not a Passing Phase*, London, Pluto Press.

LEWIS, M.M. (1968) *Language and Personality in Deaf Children*, Slough, National Foundation for Education Research.

LLWELLYN-JONES, M. (1987) 'Bi-lingualism and the education of deaf children', *Proceedings of the LASER Conference, October, 1987*, Derby. (Also Article 5.7 in D251 Reader Two)

LYNAS, W. (1986) *Integrating the Handicapped into Ordinary Schools,* London, Croom Helm. (Also Article 5.9 in D251 Reader Two)

LYNAS, W., HUNTINGTON, A. and TUCKER, I. (1988) *A Critical Examination of Different Approaches to Communication in the Education of Deaf Children*, a Ewing Foundation Publication, University of Manchester. (Also Article 5.5 in D251 Reader Two)

MANNHEIM, K. (1936) *Ideology and Utopia*, London, Routledge and Kegan Paul.

MCCORMICK, B. (1976) *A Parents Guide to Developmental Sequences and Suitable Play Activities for Hearing Impaired Children Between the Ages of Six Months and Five Years,* London, National Deaf Children's Society.

MEDOFF, M. (1982) *Children of a Lesser God*, Oxford, Amber Lane Press. (First published in 1980.)

MILES, D. (1988) *British Sign Language: A Beginner's Guide*, London, BBC Books (BBC Enterprises). (D251 Set Book)

MULKAY, M. (1979) *Science and the Sociology of Knowledge*, London, George Allen and Unwin.

MULKAY, M. (1985) *The Word and the World*, London, George Allen and Unwin.

NATIONAL UNION OF THE DEAF (1982) *Charter of the Rights of the Deaf: Part One, The Rights of the Deaf Child*, Guildford, National Union of the Deaf.

NGŨGĨ WA THIONG'O (1986) *Decolonising the Mind; The Politics of Language in American Literature*, London, James Currey.

NOBLE, W. (1978) 'Assessment of impaired hearing', in Gregory, S. and Hartley, G.M. (eds) (1990) *Constructing Deafness*, London, Pinter Publishers. (D251 Reader Two, Article 4.2)

NOLAN, M. and TUCKER, I. (1981) *The Hearing Impaired Child and the Family*, London, Souvenier Press.

PADDEN, C. (1980) 'The deaf community and the culture of deaf people', in Baker, C. and Battison, R. (eds) *Sign Language and the Deaf Community: Essays in Honour of William C. Stokoe*, Washington, National Association of the Deaf. (Also Article 2.4 in D251 Reader Two)

PADDEN, C. (1990) 'Folk explanation and language survival' in Middleton, D. and Edward, D. (eds) *Collective Remembering*, London, Sage Publications.

PADDEN, C. and HUMPHRIES, T. (1988a) *Deaf in America*, London, Harvard University Press.

PADDEN, C. and HUMPHRIES, T. (1988b) 'Learning to be deaf', in Gregory, S. and Hartley, G.M. (eds) (1990) *Constructing Deafness*, London, Pinter Publishers. (D251 Reader Two, Article 1.1)

PARRATT, D. and TIPPING, B. (1986) 'The state, social work and deafness', in Gregory, S. and Hartley, G.M. (eds) (1990) *Constructing Deafness*, London, Pinter Publishers. (D251 Reader Two, Article 7.3)

QUIGLEY, S. and PAUL, P. (1984) 'Cognition and language', in Gregory, S. and Hartley, G.M. (eds) (1990) *Constructing Deafness*, London, Pinter Publishers. (D251 Reader Two, Article 3.1)

ROBINSON, K. (1987a) *Children of Silence; The Story of Sarah and Joanne's Triumph Over Deafness*, London, Victor Gollanz.

ROBINSON, K. (1987b) 'The appointment', in Taylor, G. and Bishop, J. (eds) (1990) *Being Deaf: The Experience of Deafness*, London, Pinter Publishers. (D251 Reader One, Article 2)

ROWBOTHAM, S. (1972) *Women, Resistance and Revolution*, London, Penguin Books.

ROWBOTHAM, S. (1974) *Hidden From History: Three Hundred Years of Women's Oppression and the Fight Against It*, London, Pluto Press (second corrected impression).

SCHUCHMAN, J.S. (1988) 'Hollywood speaks: deafness and the film entertainment industry', in Gregory, S. and Hartley, G.M. (eds) (1990) *Constructing Deafness*, London, Pinter Publishers. (D251 Reader Two, Article 8.2)

SHOTTER, J. (1984) *Social Accountability and Selfhood*, Oxford, Blackwell.

SHOTTER, J. and GERGEN, K. (1989) (eds) *Texts of Identity*, London, Sage Publications.

SILO, J. (work in progress) *The Role of Deaf Teachers in the Education of Deaf Children*, MPhil in preparation, Milton Keynes, The Open University.

TAYLOR, G. (1986a) 'Social policy and deaf people', *Journal of the National Council of Social Workers with the Deaf*, vol. 2 (2), pp. 4–13.

TAYLOR, G. (1986b) 'Deaf people, ethnic minorities and social policy', in Gregory, S. and Hartley, G.M. (eds) (1990) *Constructing Deafness*, London, Pinter Publishers. (D251 Reader Two, Article 7.2)

VAN CLEVE, J.V. and CROUCH, B.A. (1989) *A Place of Their Own: Creating the Deaf Community in America*, Washington, DC, Gallaudet University Press.

VAN UDEN, A. (1975) 'Religion and language in the pre-lingual deaf', in Pokorny, D.H. (ed.) *My Eyes Are My Ears*, Collected Papers delivered at the 1st International Seminar on the Pastoral Care of the Deaf, Switzerland.

WHETNALL, E. and FRY, D.B. (1970) *Learning to Hear*, London, Heinemann.

WHORF, B. (1956) *Language, Thought and Reality*, J.B. Carroll (ed.) Cambridge, MA, MIT Press.

WILLIAMS, K. (1972) *You CAN Help Your Deaf Baby*, National College of Teachers of the Deaf.

WRIGHT, P. and TREACHER, A. (eds) (1982) *The Problem of Medical Knowledge: Examining the Social Construction of Medicine*, Edinburgh, Edinburgh University Press.

Acknowledgements

Grateful acknowledgement is made to the following sources for permission to reproduce material in this unit:

Text

Medoff, M. *Children of a Lesser God*, James T. White and Co. (USA, 1980) and Amber Lane Press (UK, 1982), © Medoff, M. (1980).

Figure

Figure 8.1 'Invitation', courtesy of Nottingham Health Authority.

Grateful acknowledgement is made to Trevor Landell for permission to use his painting on the covers and title pages throughout the units of this course.

Unit 9 Deaf People as a Minority Group: The Political Process

prepared for the course team by Paddy Ladd and Mary John

Contents

Associated study materials

Reader One, Article 10, 'Making Plans for Nigel: The Erosion of Identity by Mainstreaming', Paddy Ladd.

Reader Two, Article 6.7, 'British Sign Language Tutor Training Course', A. Clark Denmark.

Reader Two, Article 7.6, ' "We" Are Not Disabled, "You" Are', Vic Finkelstein.

D251 Issues in Deafness

Readers
Reader One: Taylor, G. and Bishop, J. (eds) (1990) *Being Deaf: The Experience of Deafness*, London, Pinter Publishers.
Reader Two: Gregory, S. and Hartley, G.M. (eds) (1990) *Constructing Deafness*, London, Pinter Publishers.

Set Books
Kyle, J. and Woll, B. (1985) *Sign Language: The Study of Deaf People and Their Language*, Cambridge, Cambridge University Press.
Miles, D. (1988) *British Sign Language: A Beginner's Guide*, London, BBC Books (BBC Enterprises). With a chapter by Paddy Ladd.

Videotapes
Video One   *Sandra's Story: The History of a Deaf Family*
Video Two   *Sign Language*
Video Three   *Deaf People and Mental Health*
Video Four   *Signs of Change: Politics and the Deaf Community*

Aims

The aims of this unit are:

1   To heighten or raise your awareness of some of the issues hotly debated within the social and political movement of Deaf people.
2   To consider the particular case for the Deaf community as a linguistic minority group.
3   To examine the case as put by one Deaf activist against the classification of Deaf people only as disabled people.
4   To explain the recent history and political activities of the Deaf community.
5   To establish the ways in which the political movement of Deaf people follows a recognizable pattern as compared with other minority groups.
6   To exemplify the importance of position, alignment and perspective in telling 'the' story of Deaf people.
7   To underline, by means of clear counterpoint, the view that professional service providers and the Deaf consumer often have quite dramatically different conceptions of what is, or is not, being achieved by intervention.
8   To raise issues about the nature of power and oppression in this area.
9   To alert you to new developments in the movement of Deaf people towards affirming their human rights.

Study guide

Week one

1 Getting started
Read the Introduction which informs you that this unit will put forward a 'new story' or, put another way, will look with quite different eyes at some of the material you have encountered earlier in the course. Having grasped that here there will be a 'new' story—'The Deaf activist's tale'—you need then to look towards the end where you will see that a second perspective is introduced in 'A political analyst's tale'. It would be useful, in order to understand the framework for this unit, to flick through the section headings before you begin.

2 Getting down to it
Having had a browse through the section headings and, by means of a careful reading of the Introduction, having established what is in store, you can then plan the remainder of your week, which should take you to the end of Section 1.3.

In this first week you should try to come to terms both with what this unit is arguing about and the nature of Deaf identity.

Week two

Week two falls into three parts in terms of approach and emphasis, and time should be spent getting to grips with Paddy Ladd's view on Deaf culture in its various very wide ramifications. Make notes as you go on how this contributes to the identity of Deaf people as a linguistic minority group. By the time you get to the end of Section 1.4 you should have a good grasp of what is being argued here.

You will now turn your attention to how it is that Deaf people see that they are oppressed in the way they claim to be—who the oppressors are and how they are alleged to oppress disabled people. We indicate in the Introduction that policies which turn out to be oppressive, or are perceived as such by Deaf activists, are not seemingly intended to be so by the perpetrator. We indicate that sometimes a benign intervention can be marginalizing and can have dire consequences when seen from the Deaf person's point of view. This may be something you could bear in mind and question as you read the examples given in Section 1.5.

In Sections 1.6 and 1.7 we will first be looking at how Deaf people have 'fought back'—how they have started, however tenuously, to organize to take responsibility for the determination of their own lives and the lives of their own community. This is an exciting part of this unit which, up to this point, tends to level all the criticisms, voice the disquiets, make the charges. Here we see Deaf people in control, working gradually towards positions of power and authority on matters that concern them.

Week three

Week three should be spent reading the political analyst's tale in Section 2 which takes a few steps back and observes the various contenders from the comparative viewpoint of strategy in other political movements. Finally, take stock of how you have felt about this unit. Did you agree with the Deaf activist's argument? Which parts of it did you feel were most compelling? If you were not convinced, try to think through why you were unable to suspend disbelief. Examine whether this unit has changed the way you think about issues in deafness.

Introduction

Unit 9 enters into the politics of its subject. We shall allow some of the fire of political fervour to counter the carefully balanced academic analysis of particular political positions and claims presented in the course. Why involve you, the students, in political arguments and accounts of political activities? To answer this it is first necessary to consider in a broad way what is meant by 'political'.

Any struggle for influence on and/or control of the decision-making process and for some degree of self-determination by groups of individuals can be regarded as political activity. Politics is about gaining, or retaining, or even losing power. It is about being valued, being influential and important and being recognized as such within accepted processes of democracy. To be forgotten, to be overlooked, to have decisions made on one's behalf is a frustration of the fundamental representative elements of the democratic process. We shall be examining here the alleged flaunting of democratic ideals experienced by many groups, including Deaf people. We will see that Deaf people are not only frustrated by miscarriages of democracy but that their access to knowledge and control of the political process itself is arbitrarily limited. This, it can be argued, distinguishes them from other marginalized groups who have relatively easy opportunity to learn about the political process.

As readers of this unit become familiar with the views of Deaf political activists they may come to understand their position, what their discontents are and the ways in which their feelings of powerlessness have arisen. To be fully literate about issues in deafness, one needs to know about these views and feelings. It will be clear to you already that many issues in deafness provoke strong feelings in educators, parents, employers and in the Deaf community itself. Can there really be said to be a *struggle* for power, however? Isn't this a bit strong? The following extract taken from the 'Conclusions and Recommendations' of the National Union of the Deaf's Charter of Rights of the Deaf Child captures some of this intensity of feeling and illustrates a position Deaf activists have adopted:

> The NUD therefore rests the first stage of its case to the United Nations, that the upbringing of deaf children and the treatment of the deaf community in the UK, fulfils Articles 2(b) to 2(e) of the UN's Convention on the Prevention and Punishment of the Crime of Genocide.

> It requests that the UN examine this report and commission an official enquiry into oralism and the true state of British Sign Language and the British Deaf Community ...

> The NUD requests that the following recommendations be considered in the enquiry:

> 1 That British Sign Language be accepted officially as a native language of the UK, as has Swedish Sign Language been accepted in Sweden.

> 2 That it is recognised that Sign Languages should be the vehicle of education of the profoundly deaf child in the UK, who should be educated bilingually in English and British Sign Language.

> 3 That the deaf community of the UK is a linguistic/ethnic minority of that country, and as such to be regarded as under the protection of the UN's International Covenant on Political and Civil Rights.

> 4 That under Article 27, the Convention on the Prevention and Punishment of the Crime of Genocide be recognised as applying to the BSL-using linguistic community of the UK.

> 5 Following the recommendation 1, that it become officially established on the British Government that the deaf child should be taught their native tongue first, and that English should be taught alongside this simultaneously so that they can become bilingual.

> 6 Following recommendation 4, any attempt to prevent the UK Government carrying out of this, or failure to implement fully, is recognised as a crime of genocide under Article 2 of the UN Convention.

7 That although the case for genocide in retrospect is strong, the perpetrators of it be not considered for immunity before the International Court of Human Rights.

8 That the only exception to the above come where particular individuals or organizations seek to actively defend and extend their policies of oralism following publication of this report. This be defined to include any individuals or authority that tries to close down a school for deaf children during the period leading up to the hearing of this report before the UN court, or pursues such policies that would be likely to result in such a closure.

(NUD, circa 1982)

A struggle for power may only be evidenced in small outcrops of activity, that wax and wane in intensity and passion. Lack of solidarity in the movement at the present time is recognized by Deaf activists, who nevertheless feel strongly about their cause. Battles easily dismissed by outsiders as little skirmishes are about crucial issues. To understand these one must see issues through the 'eyes' of the Deaf political activist. Remember Mao Tse Tsung's dictum, that 'to really understand something it is necessary to be involved in the process to change that thing'. Thus we will follow the ways in which Deaf people have undertaken activities to change a situation in which they feel frustrated and rendered virtually powerless. We will concentrate on three principal issues. These are:

1   The battle for the recognition of Deaf people's rights in the area of language, and more widely of culture.
2   The way in which the educational system mediates or acts as an obstacle to preserving and advancing this language and culture.
3   The political process itself.

The activities of Deaf activists will be compared with those of other minority rights groups. It may then be possible to identify the ways in which the particular oppressions of Deaf people have uniquely excluded them from participation in the political process.

Cautionary tales

The course contains several 'narratives', each told from a particular perspective. A narrative introduced here takes the perspective of an activist within the Deaf community presented in the passionate language of struggle, oppression, warfare and, as we have seen, even genocide, in order to raise consciousness and mobilize action within the group towards achieving equal rights or fair treatment. This is set within a narrative that has already unfolded earlier in the course, which has aimed at an 'objective' account and a measured debate. In this, various contributors have defined different positions which they have justified relative to stances adopted by other theorists and practitioners in the field. However, what one deems important depends upon one's perspective. The story of Deaf people seen through the eyes of administrators, professionals, academics, policy makers and teachers, for example, some of whom incidentally may themselves be deaf, is counterpointed here by that of the Deaf activist. We are made to feel less comfortable about the apparent achievements of the various interventions that have been described, and we sense some of the frustrations and dissatisfactions. The reader is alerted to moral issues that many of us have not thought about before.

A tale of two perspectives

The two narratives interact. If issues in deafness are treated only as matters for debate this can effectively depoliticize them. Such debates can serve to deflect attention from the reality that what is happening is about power and control, about struggles which are real and deeply felt by Deaf people. The fact that power issues are involved is obscured by the language used. The measured tones of debate can have the effect of sanitizing oppressive activities and behaviours. The use of language as a tool of depoliticization is described by E.M. Thompson in *Protest and Survive* (Smith and Thompson, 1980). He describes how nuclear warfare can be made to seem clean and wholesome, giving examples of the sanitizing effect of referring to the 'theatre' of war, to 'surgical' strikes etc.—which make the activity of killing and maiming people seem like strategic exercises rather than murders— 'clean' rather than dirty! H.T. Nash, in the same publication, writes:

> As America's involvement with the Vietnam war grew deeper the Defence vocabulary expanded and displayed an even greater imaginative and anaesthetizing flair. Bombing raids became 'surgical strikes' and the forced movement and impounding of Vietnamese citizens were part of America's 'pacification program'—terms suggesting images of the hospital operating room or a Quaker meeting. The enemy was not killed, but instead was 'taken out', 'wasted' or 'blown away' as a consequence of 'executive action' or a 'protective action/ foray'. A military ground offensive was termed 'aggressive defence' and spraying an area with machine gun fire was nothing more than 'reconnaissance by fire'.
>
> (Nash, 1980)

The language used in the course so far is a language that Deaf people see as a language of the powerful: non-contentious language used for matters which are deeply contentious and threatening in the eyes of Deaf people (the powerless). We move to what has been referred to as the 'language of power' in the way it divides people into the oppressed and the oppressor. The oppression that concerns us here arises from society's non-recognition or denial of Deaf people's language and culture. In the political mobilization of minority groups it is often the strength of feeling which starts to focus the problems and energize and animate solutions and courses of action. We aim to understand the inner feelings and workings of this political movement, and the ways in which other minority groups engage in activities aimed at bringing about social change.

Just as the story as given by the professional, the administrator, the educationalist can appear to depoliticize a deeply political issue, so too can the activists' story suggest malevolent *intent*. It is important to note that a society may have a benevolent intent towards a minority group but be oppressive by failing to understand the needs of that group, and imposing arbitrary policy solutions on it. Also, when a social policy is benign but ineffectual it may be perceived by the recipient group as oppressive. In any question of human rights it is possible to discern two strands which are mirrored in these two narratives. Many human rights imply an obligation on others to provide certain services and facilities. But, apart from these obligations of the state, there should be rights of individuals to determine their own affairs. Sometimes these two aspects are confused and those charged with providing services for the satisfaction of certain basic rights go beyond their brief and take on the responsibility of deciding for others what their needs are. It is the tension arising from this confusion that makes for polarities between the two stories.

Let us now follow the story of Deaf activists—the 'powerless'. It may cause you to re-examine some of the accounts you have already read.

1 The Deaf activist's tale

1.1 Who are we?

The oppression that we as Deaf people suffer relates to society's refusal to acknowledge us a linguistic minority group. The recognition of our own language forms a fundamental part of this. The importance of this language to our Deaf community is generally not appreciated. This is partly influenced by the fact that we as Deaf people show varying degrees of competence in using spoken language and so it is assumed by the hearing community that spoken language is what we would all naturally aspire to. This is by no means generally the case. The issue of language is further compounded by views in the hearing world, ably outlined by Lane (1984), who makes our point well: 'Only two kinds of people, after all, fail to use your language properly: foreigners and retardates'. Since we are clearly not foreigners then in the oppressor's eyes we must be seen as retardates. The analogy with foreigners is of course quite appropriate in our view. Yet the view of Deaf people as having limited intellectual ability, based largely on our competence with the language of the hearing world, is a common one.

The struggles we have been involved in go beyond a right to use our own language. They are intricately bound up with the issue of our status and identity. We do not wish to be regarded as people who are deficient in some way because many of us cannot speak or cannot hear very much. We are not impaired members of a hearing world, we are Deaf people. We *can* communicate. Our political platform is that we are not simply disabled people but fully able members of a linguistic minority group. This is the reason why we are moved to protest, anger and outrage when access to and use of our own language is blocked. Any interference with our ability to teach this language, to learn it and to use it as our first language is seen by us as an act of oppression. Many of our power struggles have, throughout history, centred on the preservation of this language. This language is the cornerstone of our proud heritage as Deaf people, is the essence of Deaf culture and is the medium of our community life and community effectiveness. We have argued throughout history that we are indeed a race, a race bound together in community by our language.

There has proved to be no easy route by which the concept of a Deaf race could be translated into political action, no straightforward way to prove to society that as Deaf people we are a race. In Unit 2 you have already learnt about John Flournoy and his attempts to set up a Deaf state. It is important to remember that Flournoy was not alone in aspiring to this and some of the dialogue of the time rehearsed the arguments as to whether or not a Deaf state was realistic or desirable. The central notion underpinning it arose constantly in the nineteenth century, which was that Deaf people had a language and culture of their own, and as such functioned more like a race than any other comparable social model.

In Unit 2 you learnt Bell's view on such a subject. In *Memoir Upon the Formation of A Deaf Variety of the Human Race* (Bell, 1884), he outlined draconian measures for 'dealing with' the deaf following his experiences in Martha's Vineyard. Bell was a fervent opponent of the idea of a 'Deaf race', and it shows how widespread the term was in those days that he used it as the basis of an article. So although the idea has had supporters, it has also had intense opponents. It is interesting to speculate why it should have attracted such a passionate reaction. In those times, of course, it was easier to conceive of a 'Deaf race', as there was a strong network of deaf schools, Deaf teachers and principals, a Deaf college and a teacher-training institute forwarded and propagated by a Deaf person, Laurent Clerc. Nevertheless, despite Bell's alarmism it was easily observed that few deaf marriages produced deaf children. In fact, the concept of a Deaf race founders on the criterion of ethnicity.

At that stage the linguistic arguments were not sufficiently scientific to be convincing. In the nineteenth century there was as yet no clear basis for accepting sign languages as natural languages. In Europe after the Milan Conference in 1880 there were actually significant shifts in political and public policy towards eliminating sign language. European Deaf people's powerlessness against such reforms were seen as ominous by Americans like Veditz who issued this warning:

> ... we American Deaf know, the French Deaf know the German Deaf know that in truth, the oral method is the poorest. Our beautiful sign language is now beginning to show the results of their attempts. They have tried to banish signs from the schoolroom, from churches, and from the earth. Yes, they have tried, so our sign language is deteriorating ... 'A new race of pharaohs that knew not Joseph' are taking over the land and many of our American schools. They do not understand signs, for they cannot sign. They proclaim that signs are worthless and of no help to the Deaf. Enemies of the sign language, they are enemies of the true welfare of the Deaf ... . As long as we have Deaf people on earth, we will have signs ... . It is my hope that all will love and guard our beautiful sign language as the noblest gift God has given to Deaf people.

(Veditz, 1913)

When, much later, in the 1960s, it was shown that sign language was indeed a language, it was possible to redefine the Deaf race in terms of a 'linguistic minority', though it was not until the late 1970s that the minority group connection was made. Arthur Dimmock, the chairman of the National Union of the Deaf (NUD), one of the few remaining Deaf people influenced by the nineteenth century Deaf attitudes, sums up the process well. As late as 1980 he was writing: 'The way to gain our rightful place as an independent and ethnic group is to get the deaf to sit on the board of crucial decision making and political processes which affects their own lives' (Dimmock, 1980).

Dimmock and other Deaf writers use 'race' and 'ethnic' as interchangeable terms. In this he was giving expression to an intuitive belief shared by many Deaf people. Being intuitive it was never thought through, and was not taken seriously by those in charge of Deaf people's lives. But by 1986, Dimmock was able to say: 'I quite like the phrase "Linguistic Minority" ... I used Ethnic Minority in the past, but it raised a lot of objections because of its alien tag' (Dimmock, 1986).

Dimmock and other Deaf writers, in using terms like 'race', 'ethnic' and finally 'linguistic minority', were trying to establish a coherent group, identifiable in some recognizable category. Rastafarians too have had similar battles for recognition, as an ethnic rather than as a linguistic minority group. They too were unable to identify the discrimination and oppression they experienced until they achieved recognition as an ethnic group. A recent ruling (reported in Equal Opportunities Review, 1989) by an industrial tribunal found that Rastafarians are an ethnic group because they show:

Δ   a long shared history

Δ   a cultural tradition of their own

Δ   a common literature

Δ   a common geographical origin or descent

Δ   a sense of being a minority and of being an oppressed group because of their particular customs.

On most of these criteria Deaf people would qualify as an ethnic minority group. It has been important to the political identity of our movement for Deaf people to identify with being Deaf and for us to define ourselves that way. Our group has also had to be defined in a way which encompasses that specific identity and its status as an oppressed minority group. Charlotte Baker-Shenk, writing about us as an oppressed group, queries what it means, in concrete terms, to state that someone is a member of an 'oppressed' group:

> It means you suffer because the dominant group denigrates your self-worth, your abilities, your intelligence and your right to be different and affirmed in your difference. It means having neither power in the institutions that impact your life, nor opportunities for self-determination. It often means a denial of your language, its worth or your opportunities to use it, and a denigration of your culture. (Consider the experiences of Black Hispanic and Native American people in the United States.) It frequently means receiving a poor

quality education, and then facing a lack of jobs and opportunities for job advancement. It often results in discrimination in housing, bank loans and medical services.

(Baker-Shenk, 1986)

We share these things with other minority groups, but it is as a linguistic minority with a collective history that we obtain group solidarity and can mobilize to try to bring about change. The general failure or refusal to recognize this history has had the effect of fragmenting the group and blocking our political activism and effectiveness.

1.2 The sources of disbelief

The major rejection of the view of Deaf people as a linguistic minority group has come from people who believe that Deaf people should primarily be regarded as disabled people and treated as such. Once considered 'disabled' we can be thought about as imperfect members of a hearing society rather than as competent members of a different linguistic society. This view is held to some extent by the lay person and is seemingly strongly held by professionals. The lay person's attitudes affect how we are regarded and responded to in society. The views that professional service providers hold about us affect how our autonomy is respected, how we are provided for, the educational opportunities we have access to, and how opinions about us are transmitted in society.

1.2.1 Lay views

We find that the public at large feel positively about having sign language on television, even throughout films and the news programmes, as a survey carried out by the Independent Broadcasting Authority showed:

> Ninety-two per cent of respondents said they had previously seen a television programme with sign language inserts. Among these, forty-four per cent said they had seen signing used in local news programmes. Nearly sixty per cent of those who had seen signing on TV thought it should be used in general programmes for any topic. Only thirty per cent thought that signing should be restricted to topics of special interest to the deaf and hard-of-hearing.

(IBA, 1984)

Yet the television professionals insist that the public would not like to see this intrude on their programmes, when they reject the campaigns of the Deaf Broadcasting Council. It is often said by Deaf people that perhaps it is the television professionals themselves who do not want the pictures on their screen rendered less attractive by sign language.

A further example of positive attitudes among the general public is the continuing electoral success of Jack Ashley MP, which further demonstrates that people do not always believe that hearing loss is a barrier to functioning intelligently in society. In 1990, a born deaf person was also elected as SDP councillor in Southwark—contrast this with the professional view which has, in effect, issued rulings with the power of law, specifically to prevent Deaf people gaining employment in a diverse range of fields, from teaching to HGV driving. Had they the power, they might well rule Deaf people ineligible to stand as Members of Parliament as well.

Even more significant are lay people's attitudes when Deaf people are more visible around their lives. We have already read of the signing in Martha's Vineyard in Unit 1. To this we can add the examples of Providence Island in the Caribbean (Woodward, 1982; Washabaugh, 1986) and a village in the Yucatan, Mexico, where the signing was so well established that it was actually a form of Mayan Sign, not Mexican Sign! Only thirteen adults and one baby out of the population of 400 were congenitally deaf but again the whole village used sign. It does not mean, as in the example above, that hearing people are surrounded by deaf people. In Martha's Vineyard as a whole the percentage of deaf people was 0.6 per cent—though in one town it was as high as 25 per cent—yet Sign was used throughout the whole island.

Moving to the present day, there are examples of parts of towns where Deaf and hearing people interact freely in everyday life. Describing the town of Fremont, California, which offers unrivalled opportunities for work for Deaf people, Oliver Sacks observes that the existence of many Deaf people in one area:

> ... has given rise to a fascinating bilingual and bi-cultural situation whereby Sign and speech are used equally. There is here not only an interface but a considerable fusion of the two cultures, so that numbers of the hearing (especially children) have started to acquire Sign, usually quite unconsciously, by picking it up rather than deliberately learning it.

(Sacks, 1989)

Sacks goes on to say: 'Thus even here [in Fremont] ... we see that the benign Martha's Vineyard situation can re-emerge' (ibid.). Given these positive examples of interaction between Deaf and hearing people, how is it that Deaf people's definitions of themselves as a linguistic minority group are not completely accepted?

The general belief persists that as deaf people are not able to hear sound, we therefore cannot hear language and thus cannot function fully in 'normal' society. It is observed, however, that we can manage, even though many of us hear little, to have limited individual one-to-one conversations with hearing people. Nevertheless, we are not seen as competent language users, in that we do not appear able to understand what people say when they talk in groups. We are also seen as excluded from watching and enjoying films and television because in the lay person's view we cannot hear the soundtrack.

◄ Activity 1
To gain some insight on this point, you might like to think back to a time when you have watched a foreign film, or a television show or a play based in an entirely different non-European culture. You may have had the benefit of subtitles but did you really feel you grasped the full significance of what was going on? ◄

In fact the obstacles to comprehension go beyond the availability of sound. The language itself and the whole context of the screenplay is based on meanings, understandings and subtle cues within a linguistic culture which is not our own. We are in effect excluded from a full appreciation of the significance of what is going on.

This does not mean that we as Deaf people are any more excluded than hearing people are when they watch a film made in and about Somalia, for example, many parts of which are baffling to them because they do not understand the culture. Much of what goes on in the media is predicated upon the culture and assumptions of a hearing world. The obstacles we as Deaf people experience in having full citizenship in the world can be seen in one of two ways which lie in different categories, as Figure 9.1 shows. How these obstacles are perceived relate to one's definition of oneself. A Deaf person within the social and political movement of Deaf people will immediately interpret the obstacles to full citizenship by Explanation B, whilst a deaf person not so aligned would possibly categorize the difficulties in the self-deprecating way outlined in Explanation A: that is, by adopting the view generally held amongst hearing people. The problems faced by Deaf people can be interpreted in these two ways. It can be thought that we have problems because we cannot hear language and sound, or that we have problems because of the position in which society has placed us, by failing to recognize and make provision for our own language and culture. We can thus define ourselves negatively in terms of obstacles in the external world, or positively in terms of our own language and culture.

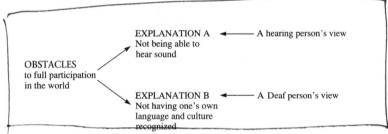

Figure 9.1   Different explanations of obstacles Deaf people face

1.2.2 The 'disability' ascription

Let us pursue further the view of disability, deficiency, impairment and handicap as conceived in Explanation A. Essentially, Deaf people do have a foot in both camps and it is because of the dual membership of the mainstream culture and of our own specific culture that difficulties in understanding our particular problems arise. Whilst disability is not an altogether appropriate model for the self-identity of Deaf people there are important parallels. Often we have chosen to align ourselves with the activities of disabled people, not particularly because we see ourselves as 'disabled', but because we too are marginalized by the same embracing legislation and are thus involved in similar struggles. In a comparable way we might show solidarity with working class, Black or ethnic marginalized groups.

◄ Reading
Now re-read Article 7.6, ' "We" Are Not Disabled, "You" Are' by Vic Finkelstein in
Reader Two. ◄

Vic Finkelstein's article reinforces the commonly held views that Deaf
people share the problems of disabled people. He states: 'I believe that the
meaning of disability is determined by the way our society is organized.' He
points out that disabled people, too, wish to distance themselves from the
label 'disabled' with its negative economic and social connotations. He says
that, despite this wish, there are two contemporary service approaches
which keep alive the general public image of disabled people as a uniform
social group, based upon the medical model and the administrative model.
He regards these service approaches as contributing most to the general
public image of disabled people.

Deaf people have been grouped with disabled people in the thinking behind
both these models. We have, therefore, sometimes aligned ourselves with
disabled people. We have joined in their crusades to throw off professional
imperialism in defining our distinct needs. In common with disabled
people, we see the source of our problems arising from the way society is
organized; that is, in the way in which professional, environmental,
financial, legal and information systems assume able-bodied people. As we
have seen, there is a powerful argument that it is the way in which the
world has been organized around able-bodied people's abilities and
requirements that disables many impaired people and, by extension, Deaf
people.

Sign language is specifically not sound based, and so uses primarily one
communication channel whereas most languages use two. This is important
in understanding how constructivist arguments apply to modes of language
as much as to modes of mobility. Language does not need to be sound
based. Nevertheless, some aspects of the world are inescapably sound based,
such as traffic, birdsong and music. In common with social constructivist
models of disability, however, one can argue that the importance attached
to certain sounds for the purposes of surviving and functioning in a social
world has been determined by hearing people. It is conceivable and
perfectly possible to live in a world so designed that crucial emphasis was
not given to sound-based features.

Our argument is slightly different from that of disabled people in general in
that we feel we have a perfectly adequate language system and we wish to
have it recognized and provided for. The point of departure, from our point
of view, is that we do not want mainstream society to re-structure so that
we can be *part* of it. Rather, we wish for the recognition of our right to
exist as a linguistic minority group within that society. If we were to take
the position outlined in the article by Finkelstein, we would be pressing for
mainstream society to become bilingual. That in a perfect world would be
wonderful but is no more realistic than asking everyone to know a number
of European languages. No, what we fundamentally require and crusade for
is the recognition of our rightful status as a linguistic minority group, and,
bound up with that, the recognition of our language and the right to learn
and use it in an education system we control. This is the central issue
around which we organize and campaign.

Labelling us as 'disabled' demonstrates a failure to understand that we are not disabled in any way within our own community. We see a refusal to recognize this culture fully, to become excited by its wholeness, its dynamism, its life. Many disabled people see Deaf people as belonging, with them, outside the mainstream culture. We, on the other hand, see disabled people as 'hearing' people in that they use a different language to us, from which we are excluded, and see them as being members of society's culture, as 'consumers' when active participation is restricted by society's attitude to 'its own'. Deaf people have their own culture and a different thinking process stemming from a different language. Our American Deaf cousins have learnt a considerable amount from the activities of disabled people generally about how to organize and to become effective agents of social change. By being subsumed within the 'disability group' we have lost out in the distribution of resources. When large sums of money are set aside for 'the disabled', it appears that the government has been generous. If, however, that constituency is broken down into its various groups, it becomes clear that the sums are pitifully small, and the share made available to Deaf people, for interpretation services for example, woefully inadequate.

We believe as Deaf activists that if a person considers him- or herself to be 'Deaf', aligns him- or herself with our campaigns, or takes a part in our struggles to preserve our unique culture, then that person can come to know what being Deaf means. Our feeling is that to be involved in the political struggles gives our members the full knowledge, commitment and allegiance of the partisan.

People who think of deafness as a pathology have vigorously sought ways to prevent and cure deafness. They have devised intervention programmes for deaf children of younger and younger ages. People who are culturally Deaf hold a very different perspective. Our immediate response is to oppose talk about prevention, cure, early intervention. Rather than prevention, many Deaf parents want to have Deaf children. We are interested in passing on our rich heritage to Deaf children who are fine, just as we are fine. We do not want or need to become hearing in order to consider ourselves normal. For us, early intervention does not mean ear phones, amplifiers and training a child to appear as hearing as possible. Instead, a really good early intervention programme would offer deaf children and hearing parents early exposure to sign language and many opportunities to interact with Deaf adults.

As Bienvenu writes about the protest at Gallaudet:

> The Gallaudet uprising focused much attention on Deaf people. Now, a year later, some organizations for the Deaf have started to identify as disabled in order to have more political 'clout'. I am questioning that strategy. Although as individuals, we may support the struggles of disabled people, we need to ask ourselves who benefits when we attempt to work in coalition with disability groups. Do we have the same goals? More and more Deaf people have organized to obtain formal credit for ASL [American Sign Language] as a foreign language. How can we fight for official recognition of ASL and allow ourselves as 'communication disordered' at the same time? We need to stop and think. We need not accept any other label than Deaf. We can succeed, as we have shown in the past, on our own or by joining with other

minority language groups. Our goals for education are similar; our concerns about oppression and lack of understanding are similar. Most important, we are similar because although our numbers are small, we are proud of our language, culture and heritage. Disabled, we are not!

(Bienvenu, 1989)

1.3 Dual category membership

As we have seen, it can be technically correct to include Deaf people with disabled people, and there can be reasons why it is contingently useful for us to be included. This seems to be at odds with our own thinking as Deaf people. Yet there is a way forward. To quote the NUD's Charter of Rights of the Deaf Child:

> Why are Deaf people a Linguistic Minority? ...
>
> It is possible to be a member of both a disabled minority and an ethnic minority, as any black person knows. Deaf people are people with disabilities who are oppressed as a linguistic minority. This suggestion of dual-category membership, that Deaf people should be included in legislation that covers both linguistic minorities and disabled people seems rather obvious. Yet, as we shall see later, there are still problems of accepting this.
>
> (NUD, circa 1982)

If Deaf people are seen as disabled, then in what sense do other disabled groups have a culture which is specifically theirs in the way Deaf culture is ours? Yet sharing the same problems and oppressive interventions in the case of disability does not constitute 'a culture'. Take, for example, the 'grey panther' movement in the USA. Although there are common forms of oppression of elderly people involved, this common mission to end such oppression has not of itself given birth to a culture. A culture is created out of shared *values* rather than merely by the way one particular group is seen by other people. A political group, for example, does not of itself constitute a culture in that choosing to be together culturally is a *social* as well as a political thing.

1.4 The concept of Deaf culture

If you travel abroad you have to be careful to respect other people's values. This is one of the most difficult aspects of culture to understand, because one does not already realize one has inherited values. People tend to believe that the way they grew up is the right way of doing things and are often intolerant of other cultural standards, which can manifest themselves in attitudes about cleanliness, the proper role of the family, or colonization, to give just three examples of the sweeping range of cultural values. Examples from the Deaf community span a similarly wide range, ranging from the values emphasized in residential schools (even if they follow an oral regime) or by generations of Deaf families, to attitudes about behaving in ways that will not cause hearing people to deride us, including learning to 'pass' in

16

the dominant culture. Many Deaf people are bi-cultural—they can operate and take on the values of both the hearing world and our own Deaf culture, although at times these are in conflict. We are also, to some degree, influenced by our national culture.

Once the linguistic status of Sign was confirmed and believed, the concept of culture could be examined. Even though signing is in widespread use, Deaf culture often does not receive the media attention it deserves and which would help in dispelling some of the 'disability' images of deafness that remain in the popular consciousness and underline its cultural significance. Take Oliver Sacks' description of the Deaf march to the Capitol on 11 March 1988:

> For here are a thousand or more people signing freely, in a public place—not privately at home, or in the enclosure of Gallaudet—but openly and unselfconsciously and beautifully before the Capitol.

> The press had reported all the speeches, but missed what is equally significant. They fail to give the watching world *an active vision of the fullness and vividness, the unmedical life of the deaf.*
>
> (Sacks, 1989, our emphasis)

Whilst sign language has a long history, the term 'culture' has itself only been used in connection with Deaf people in the last few years in the Deaf community in England. Although there are several ways in which culture can be broken down into categories and analysed, we have used a combination of what we regard as salient elements for analysis in this unit. These include: language and traditions; rules for behaviour; values; group norms; identity.

1.4.1 Culture and sign language

> To reject ASL is to reject the deaf person ... (for) ASL is a personal creation of deaf persons as a group ... it is the only thing we have that belongs to deaf people completely.
>
> (B. Kannapell, in Sacks, 1989)

In all societies, language is the means by which traditions, values, norms, rituals and codes of behaviour are conveyed. More than this, however, languages have an active, dialectical role in helping to shape and determine how people think, feel and aspire. This is what gives a people their personal identity.

A language is, therefore, saturated in cultural attitudes, it is an essential part of the transmission and preservation of the culture, and BSL is no different. Here are some examples of how we use BSL to convey attitudes: Deaf people's sign for themselves involves putting fingers over both ears and the mouth, giving a 'deaf-mute' signed appearance. However, we will not tolerate anyone referring to us as 'deaf and dumb', when English words are used. Sign construction reveals some of our cultural attitudes too. The sign for 'integration' is made in its root form, with two hands coming together to form one 'stream'. However, we more widely sign it in such a way that it carries two extra levels of meaning: one, that deaf children are vastly outnumbered by the hearing pupils of 'integrated' schools; two, a slight twist of the right hand as it goes across the left acts as a kind of poetic pun, since that movement is found in other signs which mean 'to oppress'. It is through such language creativity that we feel cultures express and pass on new ideas and concepts.

1.4.2 Culture and tradition

Once a culture goes beyond a single group lifetime, its values and beliefs start to manifest themselves as traditions. The Deaf community is no exception. We Deaf people have a historical dimension to our lives. The Gallaudet strike of 1988, for example, underlined the historical consciousness of the movement. This was not just a demonstration in the 1980s but linked the campaign to the history of Deaf people, as evidenced in one picket's banner, 'Laurent Clerc wants Deaf Prez. He is not here but his *spirit* is here. Support us'. There was a sense of cultural continuity.

Roger Carver suggests that cultures do change, such that some become more distinctive and stronger, while others weaken or disappear completely:

> On the other hand cultures do die out. One way of accomplishing this is by using brutal methods. The Spanish succeeded in wiping out the ancient Aztecs and Inca civilizations of Latin America. This is called genocide (meaning the destruction of an entire people or culture). Another way to destroy a culture is much slower but deadlier: oppression or assimilation. Oppression occurs when a dominant culture tries to control another and to suppress its old ways. However, oppression often backfires as it can make the oppressed culture stronger and more stubborn. The most deadly way to kill off a culture is through assimilation or being absorbed by the dominant culture. Why is it the most dangerous when it looks like the most comfortable way? It creeps up on an unsuspecting culture and catches it unawares. Before long it is too late to reverse the trend, resulting in loss of identity and the death of a culture.
>
> (Carver, 1988)

Carver believes that Deaf culture evolved and grew over the years largely through diffusion, in that it borrowed a lot from the hearing world. He believes that a good example of diffusion is Japan, in that the Japanese borrowed a great many things from the American culture over a period of about 100 years and changed considerably as a result. The Japanese did not lose their culture, however, they kept their traditions, and their language grew mostly by borrowing from other languages. In the case of Deaf culture, however, the process of diffusion has not continued uninterrupted. In England, much of the historical consciousness and the steady growth of the culture has been damaged by oralism. Nevertheless, Deaf social life that evolves around British Deaf Association (BDA) rallies and deaf school reunions, where some of the schools date back to the 1830s, has plenty of scope to express traditions.

1.4.3 Rules for behaviour

You may understand this if you think of what you have to remember to do or not to do when visiting another country. You have already learnt some of the Deaf rules in Unit 2. If you take the example of touch, however, you will find even more complex rules. For example, if you are 'talking' to someone, and a third person touches your arm to get attention, the quality of the touch tells you about the urgency of the message, whether you must know the information now, or simply that a person is letting you know they have arrived and would like a word with you later. When it comes to understanding the rules for non-verbal behaviour, a hearing person's assumptions tend generally to be that all non-verbal behaviour is the same as in their particular hearing culture. This is a mistaken assumption and can lead to all sorts of misunderstandings.

1.4.4 Group norms

Cultural norms are the practical expression of values—they are the acting out of the values. Usually this is not easily noticed until people differ from the norm. In our Deaf community, such norms include the following:

- Δ In conversation, if you are Deaf you will quickly be asked what school you attended, and if you did not attend one of the deaf schools, you can meet with a puzzled and slightly disapproving reaction, as if your status as a Deaf person is briefly questioned.
- Δ Fear of behaving in ways that will cause hearing people to deride us manifests itself in various norms. There is a strong conservatism in the Deaf culture in Britain. A small example was seen in the negative reaction of many deaf people to Clive Mason when he first became the presenter of 'See Hear', the BBC magazine programme for deaf and hard-of-hearing people. His informal screen manner led many to worry about how they would be perceived by hearing people as a result, since they were unfamiliar with the cultural shift of the 1960s that allowed hearing people in Britain to be more informal.

1.4.5 Culture and identity

All cultures have rules for identifying and being accepted as members of their society. Deaf culture seems to have a complex set of rules for identity and acceptance, as you have already learned in Unit 2. If someone has not been to a deaf school or is the deaf child of hearing parents, there is often a long drawn-out process of developing one's Deaf identity and becoming accepted into the Deaf community. Similarly, the status of hearing children of Deaf parents has an ambiguous relationship with Deaf culture and Deaf identity.

1.4.6 Other cultural manifestations

Culture is also what societies create and make: artifacts and so on. It is this dimension that caused many people to deny that Deaf people had a culture. Where was Deaf cooking, or pottery, or architecture, they argued. There are indeed various Deaf art forms. You will have seen the poem in Video Two, and will learn more about Deaf art in Unit 10.

The term 'culture' has wider meanings than just its art, craft and artifacts. The culture has to be socially embedded. Deaf communities do also have this dimension, in Deaf clubs, maintaining Deaf magazines and so on.

In conclusion then, we can see that Deaf culture has a considerable depth. As research into the culture grows, and our confidence and pride likewise, more of it will become explicit. For now, it remains to restate that the concept of dual category membership can only become clearer and more visible to the hearing world as such work is made explicit and disseminated into political arenas.

1.5 Agencies of oppression

1.5.1 Medicine

Deaf people are at the mercy of medical professionals from the time they are first diagnosed as deaf. Relationships with the medical profession from the moment of diagnosis have had two important consequences for Deaf people. One is that, from a professional viewpoint, medical diagnosis and assessment have reinforced the notion of deaf people as disabled people on account of their impaired hearing. Second, being 'patients' of the medical system, Deaf people have been victims of all the vagaries of that system in terms of power, authority and control, and colluding with the 'authority' of that system has been a host of other professionals.

If one classifies Deaf people in terms of 'deficit', then the search for a 'cure' is deemed important. If Deaf people are imperfect hearing people, so this form of argument goes, then making their hearing perfect is seen as surely the solution to their problems. Yet a 'cure' in the world of Deaf people is a subject of great debate. For example, a surgical procedure has been developed which makes it possible to implant electrodes ('cochlear implants') into the inner ear. This procedure is seen by Deaf people and by many doctors as essentially an experimental technique, concerning which there is no certainty either about the suitability of patients, the outcome of the operation, or its usefulness to the patients. Basically, the technique can give a totally deaf person a sensation of sound. But this is not sound as hearing people know it, as, since June 1984, no recipient of such an operation has been able to understand speech without visual clues. Cochlear implants have attracted great hostility from nearly all Deaf people. The implant is different from a hearing aid in that it is implanted inside the head and body and cannot be easily removed. There are even possibly some long-term dangers in that medical experts have not been able to rule out negative effects from long-term electrical stimulation. The point at issue here is that the Deaf community believe that medically there is no requirement to operate. Deafness is neither a disease nor an illness, nor does it bring any physical pain.

We in the Deaf community do not feel it proper for us to object to the operation for consenting deafened adults as such people are old enough to decide for themselves. Ethically, however, we feel it is immoral for such 'experiments' to be carried out on deaf children, as is currently happening. We feel that the child should decide for itself when it is old enough, whether to be experimented on—the parents' decision alone is not sufficient. The hearing parent may have little insight into what it means to be Deaf and little or no contact with Deaf people who could explain their own realities. We feel these surgical interventions should be outlawed as a breach of civil liberties.

So, here, as Deaf activists, we identify two confusions. First there is the confusion of the service provider, in not just providing services—in this case medical operations—but in going on to infringe civil liberties by making choices for children about changes in their cultural status: that is, attempting to make them hearing children rather than Deaf children. Second, it is a confusion to think of 'deafness' as a disability—an impaired bodily part that must, if at all possible, be put 'right'. Outsiders often think it incredible that Deaf people should even consider turning down the possibility of 'hearing'. (What were your reactions to the information that many Deaf mothers would actually choose to have a Deaf baby?) The medical model of understanding deafness has, in sum, been regarded by many Deaf people as a major obstacle to the acceptance of their status as a linguistic minority group.

1.5.2 Parents as mediators

ITQ
Imagine you grew up in a family with whom you could not communicate. What do you think the effects would be:

(a) in practical terms;

(b) in emotional terms?

There is, of course, no correct answer to the questions posed in this ITQ, but they provide a way of considering the significance of communication for family life. It is likely that the more you reflected upon the question, the more complex the issues seemed. You may have first queried the meaning of 'not communicate': does this imply nothing, no pointing to indicate, smiling to reassure, using force to restrain? Even in the more limited sense of no communication through language, the consequences seem far reaching. The practical implications are many and you are likely to have had your own ideas. The emotional implications are more complex and you may have thought about the role of communication in establishing relationships and identity. In the context of this unit, of course, the question concerns communication within a hearing family with a deaf member, and the consequences for the deaf person when the family does not sign.

A problem has been the medical influence on the well-meaning hearing parents of deaf children who have been persuaded, in the interests of getting their child to appear as 'normal' as possible, to use an oral approach and thus they have become deeply resistant to the child learning to sign. This carries social messages not just about signing *per se* but the way it represents their child being taken away from them by joining a culture they do not understand and from which they feel excluded.

◀ Reading
Now re-read Article 10, 'Making Plans for Nigel: The Erosion of Identity by Mainstreaming' by Paddy Ladd in Reader One. ◀

Often, innocently, or on an ill-informed basis, parents have, therefore, become agents of oppression too, in colluding with the system, and we as Deaf activists are rarely able to make contact with them to put our point of view. Those who do become enlightened realize that to cease being mediators of an oppressive regime they will have to take on an immense amount of work. According to the Action Alliance of Parents of the Deaf, in Fremont, California, this would be:

> ... an on-going crisis in which ordinary parents must become educational experts, cultural anthropologists, advocates, litigators. Parents of deaf children should expect to take on, at one time or another, the State Department of Education, the Judicial system, relatives, the US Government, the Deaf Education establishment, and the odd person at the super-market (who asks 'does that sweet little child lipread?').
>
> (Action Alliance of Parents of the Deaf, 1986)

1.5.3 The education system

As you have already read, following the 1880 Milan Congress oralist educators took control of the education of deaf children, when teacher training colleges were set up which banned sign language. There then developed a group of 'experts' on the education of the deaf. Deaf people were largely excluded and new difficulties were put in the way of their training to be teachers of the deaf. The government approached these 'experts', rather than Deaf people themselves, for advice. These experts took on the business of deciding what was best for Deaf people, even though they had little inside knowledge and understanding.

A real understanding of what has happened has been obscured, moreover, by the subtle evolution of a professional language in Deaf education which has clouded concepts of cultural struggle. For instance, in the literature you will read about the 'debates between manualists and oralists', as if only a polite academic disagreement was involved, and in current policy discussions about integration you will find the phrase 'school placement according to the individual needs of the child'. (This apparently liberal oralist position conveniently omits to mention the absence of sign interpreters, Deaf teachers and Deaf culture from the choices available!) This is the sanitization of language that we referred to in the Introduction. The use of 'innocent' terms in the area of our education deflects attention from the real politics.

Initial dissent from developments following the Milan Congress and the 1880 Education Act, was signalled by the setting up of national organizations all over Europe by Deaf people to defend our language and way of life. The BDA in England was founded for this reason in 1890, though the precipitating events have only in 1990 just been remembered by the movement. A sample of quotations from Deaf people at the time reveals that they were under no illusions as to what was about to happen:

The Chinese women bind their babies' feet to make them small ... .
And the people who prevent sign language being used in the
education of the deaf ... are denying the deaf their free mental growth
through natural expression of their ideas, and are in the same class of
criminals.

(J.S. Long, 1890, in Lane, 1984, our emphasis)

Both in this and in many other examples, you will find oralism described as
crime. You will shortly see the full range of damage done to the Deaf
community which reinforces this concept of a crime. In 1913, a film was
made by Deaf people (when silent films in general had barely begun!) to
preserve sign for posterity, in case oralism continued to spread:

For the last thirty-three years, the French Deaf people have watched
with tear-filled eyes and broken hearts this beautiful language of signs
snatched away from their schools. For the last thirty-three years they
have striven and sought to reinstate signs in the schools, but for
thirty-three years their teachers have cast them aside and refused to
listen to their pleas. But their teachers would much rather listen to the
worthless, cruel hearted demands of people who think they know all
about their thoughts and souls, their feelings, desires, and needs. It is
like this in Germany also.

(Veditz, 1913)

Cultural oppression legalized
A major piece of recent legislation was the 1981 Education Act, which
enforced the idea of mainstreaming. The policy of 'integration' was seen by
Deaf people within the movement as a policy of assimilation: 'This
legislation thus endorsed the genocide of the deaf community by breaking
up its roots. So-called integration has become Oralism's Final Solution'
(NUD, circa 1982).

The powerlessness felt consequent to the Act was exacerbated by the way in
which the Act had itself been developed with allegedly little or no proper
consultation with Deaf people. The Act was preceded by the Warnock
Report, which slipped by largely without much Deaf input. That some Deaf
people knew what the Report implied can be seen from Figures 9.2 and 9.3.

This again raises questions about the extent to which the oppression we as
Deaf activists campaign against is indeed intentional or whether Deaf people
are simply victims of an uncomprehending bureaucracy.

1.6 Active dissent

Deaf organizations, whilst outraged at every turn, have been slow to
respond through *formal* legal channels. It was not until 1982 that the
National Union of the Deaf approached the United Nations with a set of
proposals (extracts from which began this unit) that:

1   Deaf people and thus deaf children be treated as a linguistic minority.

2   They be accorded protection by rights governing linguistic minorities.

No 23
NOVEMBER
15p

NULD NEWSLETTER

EDITORS:-
BRIAN DAVIES
P O'TOOLE
ART EDITOR
CHRIS MARSH

PUBLISHED BY THE NATIONAL UNION OF THE DEAF.

ALERT !

DANGER TO THE DEAF COMMUNITY

ALL OVER THE U.K., ORALISTS ARE PUTTING MORE AND MORE DEAF CHILDREN INTO HEARING SCHOOLS, AND FORCING DEAF SCHOOLS TO CLOSE

IF THEY ARE NOT STOPPED, THERE WILL BE NO DEAF COMMUNITY LEFT.

WHAT DO THEY SAY?

ORALIST A. "WORK ON SIGN LANGUAGE IS A WASTE OF TIME AND MONEY. IN FUTURE THERE WILL BE BETTER HEARING AIDS, AND THUS NO SUCH THING AS A DEAF PERSON."

ORALIST B. "ONCE DEAF CHILDREN ARE INTEGRATED INTO HEARING SCHOOLS, THERE WILL BE NO MORE DEAF COMMUNITY."

WE KNOW THIS IS RUBBISH, BUT THEY ARE SUCCEEDING IN FOOLING PARENTS AND TEACHERS. WE MUST LET THEM KNOW THE TRUTH.

WHAT CAN YOU DO ?

WRITE TO NEWSLETTER AND OFFER YOUR HELP NOW*!*

Figure 9.2

NEWSLETTER
PUBLISHED BY THE
National Union of the Deaf

EDITOR:
B. Davies.

No. 35

IN 2110 ANCESTORS OF THE PRESENT DEAF MAY COME ACROSS THIS GRAVESTONE

R.I.P.

BRITISH DEAF
COMMUNITY
SUCCESSFULLY
ANNIHILATED
BY THE ORALISTS
2080 A.D.
PRAISED BE THE LORD

SEE EDITORIAL PAGE 2.

Figure 9.3

Figures 9.2 and 9.3 Covers from NUD newsletters published in the early 1980s
(Source: courtesy of the National Union of the Deaf)

3   Oralism was actually breaking laws governing linguistic minorities.

4   Oralism should itself be made illegal.

These proposals were made to the United Nations as the United Nations Charter of Rights of the Disabled was found not to reply to language issues such as oralism, and as a result, in the absence of properly ratified codes of behaviour, Deaf people's rights were being severely eroded.

This bold move failed, but the World Federation of the Deaf (WFD) has taken up negotiations of step 1 with the United Nations, so this route is still possible. The Deaf community also tried invoking the United Nations Declaration of the Rights of the Child (adopted by the United Nations in 1959) in the NUD Charter of Rights of the Deaf Child which indicated comprehensively the way in which denying the child access to his or her rightful language meant that in a number of substantial ways the UN Declaration was being broken. There were also further appeals to the United Nations Convention on the Prevention and Punishment of Genocide. The argument was detailed but focused principally on the view that:

> The British Government unwittingly left the door open to genocide when it allowed local authorities to implement the ill-considered integration policies derived from the Warnock Report. Since implementation of integration of deaf children into hearing schools causes the breaking up of the deaf community at its roots, the authorities are inflicting on deaf children conditions of life that would bring about the destruction, not only of the deaf community in the coming future, but deaf children's rightful language and culture. ... Through the implementation of integration, deaf schools are being effectively forced to close and therefore children of one ethnic/ linguistic minority group that is deaf people are being *forcibly transferred to another group* that is hearing people.
>
> (NUD, circa 1982, our emphasis)

We are angry, very angry, because it is clear to Deaf people that integration really will have consequences tantamount to genocide. We share similar sentiments about assimilation into the dominant culture of the hearing world as black South Africans have had about integration into the dominant white culture, as so ably expressed by Steve Biko thus:

> Does this mean I am against integration? If by integration you understand a breakthrough into white society by blacks, an assimilation and acceptance of blacks into an already established set of norms and code of behaviour set up by whites, YES I am against it. I am against the superior-inferior-white-black stratification that makes the white a perpetual teacher and the black a perpetual pupil (and a poor one at that). I am against the intellectual arrogance of white people that makes them believe that white leadership is a *sine qua non* ... in the country and that whites are the divinely appointed pace setters in progress ... if on the other hand by integration you mean there shall be participation by all members of society, catering for the full expression of self in a freely changing society as determined by the will of the people, then I am with you.
>
> (Biko, 1970)

Participation and self-determination by all members of society through the recognition and facilitation of sign language and thus the emancipation of Deaf culture are seemingly only a dream at the moment. Small gains are being made, however. The European section of the World Federation of the Deaf succeeded in getting EEC legislation to recognize the twelve sign languages of the member states as official languages within the EEC, and sign language as Deaf people's first language. But the individual countries are still resisting ratifying this legislation. There are many possibilities for the Deaf community here, but most them are culturally based, not medically based—a unique step forward.

1.6.1 The conspiracy of silence

By the creation of 'Experts', society absolves its responsibilities for deaf, disabled, mentally or physically ill people. Thus, whoever is an Expert can have total control over a deaf child's development, since society will not intervene to argue with the Experts. This has been clearly described in the NUD's Charter of Rights, which has termed the Experts 'the Protectors':

> Over the past two decades, deaf people have cried out for their right to equal opportunities and policy making and decisions affecting their own destiny. All their pleas were brushed aside by the Protectors—that is Oralists, legislators, educators and administrators who work in connection with the deaf. These Protectors regard themselves as experts on deafness and deaf people, even to the extent that they regard the deaf as knowing little about themselves ... The Protectors' stranglehold on deaf education, deaf children and their parents has led to the destruction of the natural process of deaf children's development into first class deaf adults. They have created a group of people groomed to play an inferior role in society.
>
> (NUD, circa 1982)

Thus the dissent of Deaf people from all developments associated with oralism has been vigorous and strong, but we have met all too often with stonewalling and, even worse, orchestrated silence. The results of oralism in literacy terms were discussed in Unit 4. In political terms it marked the Great Divide between the hearing professional educator and Deaf people. As early as 1896, there was a warning from an Italian delegate to the World Congress of the Deaf in Geneva that, '[Italy is] weeping at the sight of so many poor deaf-mutes who leave school speaking like parrots with no understanding of what they are saying'. Moreover, such information as has been gathered seems to have been received with a degree of equanimity that has been seen by Deaf people as evidence of informed hearing society's indifference to the plight of deaf children. The following extracts are from the minutes of a meeting between the Department of Education and Science (DES) and the National Union of the Deaf on 22 September 1987, held principally to discuss the role of the DES in deaf education, and the training of teachers of the deaf, including deaf teachers. At this meeting the NUD representatives invited an 'official view' by the DES of academic standards in deaf education. In this latter context the following comment was made:

> HMI Mrs. X said that in her opinion it was a *great achievement* for some hearing impaired pupils to have reached a reading age of eight

and a half on leaving school, and it should be remembered that in the hearing world too there were many examples of pupils underachieving.

(Extracts from the official minutes of the meeting, our emphasis)

Mainstreaming seems to be producing even more alarming results, this time not only from the literacy viewpoint, but also from the question of damage to the child's psyche. Some members of oppressed minority groups, such as ethnic minorities, are very much on the political agenda even if they continue to be oppressed. Deaf people, because they are not regarded as a linguistic minority group, are not on such agendas. In the case of other recognized oppressed groups, people are now sufficiently aware of discriminatory practices as to be on the look out for abuse and to be sensitive to allegations of it. In such groups such massive underachievement as that referred to above would not be reported without a shocked response and a call for detailed further enquiries.

This is not so in the case of the Deaf group. When we draw attention to mass illiteracy such claims are ignored. Moreover, the ascription 'disabled', whilst regarded as quite inappropriate by Deaf people in the context of education, does mean that it is regarded as possible to hide what is going on, through lowered expectations of the deaf child, as a result of this labelling process. The movement is frustrated by its knowledge of this damage and society's denial of its existence.

More and more deaf children are entering residential deaf schools for the first time as late as the age of eleven. Such deaf children have previously been mainstreamed and as a consequence isolated from other deaf children in their early school life. By eleven it becomes clear even to the oralists that such children simply would not survive in a secondary school. Consider the following account:

> My colleague and I went to visit a deaf school Open Day. The school had allowed signing for about a year or so, and we visited happy class after happy class of children, teachers and parents. Then we came upon a class of seven or so children sitting almost blankly. We asked the teacher who they were, and she said they were one of two classes of children transferred from mainstream at age eleven. These children were about twelve years old. My colleague and I tried to communicate with them by BSL, by Signed English, and orally. We could not make them understand even the simplest things. The nearest comparison we could think of was with autistic children. After suggesting to the teacher that she begin right back at pre-school level with BSL and work upwards from there, we took our leave, sick at heart.
>
> (Personal communication, in a letter received by one of the authors, 1982)

Nine years have elapsed since then (as we write in 1991) and nothing seems to have happened to change things, let alone the law which created this. Still no one talks about these children. Not even the pro-sign teachers working with them, nor the national organizations for and of the deaf, have breathed a word that such things are going on. When, as Deaf activists, we are challenged to identify such schools and our sources of information, our refusal is frequently interpreted as an indication that such accounts are fabricated. It is not appreciated that it is the schools which refuse us permission to reveal our sources. One of the reasons that Deaf people themselves sometimes show some reluctance to reveal sources is that, in such a highly charged, political and delicate situation, the informant may be placed in a difficult position if his or her identity were known. In the particular arena we are considering now, however, such accounts coming from us, for many of which we do have documentary evidence, are seen as simply Deaf people's scandalmongering in a movement trying to score political points. The silence that greets our information and our shocking finding is not, however, regarded as a conspiracy of silence by the establishment, only by us.

The NUD tried to get schools to expose what they were finding. In response, one letter from a head teacher said that he felt it better to say nothing about what was happening as he did not wish to disturb parents. In that case, parents' feelings are more important than a child's mental health, yet all through this century Deaf people have had to struggle to recover from various degrees of such psychological damage.

1.6.2 Education as the cultural battleground

It is said that the first casualty of any war is 'truth'. In the 'battleground' of education the truth that is initially lost is the 'truths' Deaf people have about themselves: truths that have been central to the consciousness and activity of Deaf people in terms of their rights as equal citizens. Why is it that education is so important for Deaf people? It has a particular importance not just as education does for every child, but in quite particular ways which affect the Deaf adult's political effectiveness:

1   Deaf culture differs from other hearing cultures in that it is passed on, not from families (except the small percentage with Deaf parents), but at the deaf school, since this is where deaf children first really meet each other.

2   Hearing children in an oppressed culture still have access to the society around them. Any child or adult's understanding of society is completely dependent on their acquiring basic language and communication, with their parents, their teachers, their peers and the rest of society. Deaf people do not have this access unless people either use sign language, or the deaf person learns to read the language of that society. We have already seen that the latter is a major problem under oralism. Without adequate education the deaf child is almost totally deprived of basic socialization knowledge, and even a basic psychological wholeness. Given the oralist state of deaf schools, the only real source of information for those two processes comes from the children's peers. This is why the comparatively healthy state of Deaf children from Deaf families is important to other deaf children, as the former have more of that information and share it in school time. Furthermore, deaf people understandably are more dependent on reading if cut off from society's spoken information and, as a consequence, they are often rendered politically passive by this isolation.

If one imagines generation after generation of deaf children leaving school without adequate literacy, education or socialization and with disturbed psychological development, it is easy to see that this must affect Deaf culture in some way, and not only this, but pride in being Deaf and from the political activism that surrounds that. The first Deaf author, Desloges, gave some insight into the difference being able to communicate made in his own development:

> Therefore, when a deaf person encounters other deaf people more highly educated than he, as I myself have experienced, he learns to combine and improve his signs, which had hitherto been unordered and unconnected. In intercourse with his fellows he promptly acquires the supposedly difficult art of depictions and expressing all his thoughts, even those most independent of the senses, using natural signs with as much order and precision as if he understood the rules of grammar. Once again I must be believed, for I have been in this situation myself and speak only from my own experience.
>
> (Desloges, 1779)

Facility in signing and close contact with other Deaf people means the deaf person is strengthened by his or her own culture. Without contact with Deaf culture the young deaf person has no positive images of competent, exciting and capable Deaf people to identify with—no role models. The opportunities to develop such links and identification are very important not only for the individual's development but also for the very continuation of the whole culture, which is in danger of losing these young people. Because of the steadily diminishing awareness of their own culture, Deaf people often could not really believe that they had a language of their own equal to spoken languages. This has had an effect on several aspects of the culture, notably its art forms, which are the ways in which a culture inevitably shares and develops its ideas, through its forms of poetry, story telling, song and literature:

1   Until very recently, Deaf culture had lost its ability to create art about itself. There were no plays or poetry that were not just performances of hearing plays and poetry.

2   Then, the devaluing of sign language meant that, in these forms, BSL was never used, but instead there was a form of signing in English that rendered the performances almost unintelligible to a deaf audience. It was as if the performers were just performing for their own pleasure.

3   The loss of awareness and pride in one's own language meant that story telling, which, whilst integral to Deaf culture, is implicit and thereby largely unconscious, became a less significant activity. Stories that were told were simply to entertain. The wider cultural values which used to inform the stories, and were thereby transmitted and reinforced by them, become much less involved. The stories are rarely now vehicles for passing on our culture.

4   Literature as a written art form has very limited scope to develop when its audience cannot read. Thus this field has been almost totally stunted by the restricted literacy of many Deaf people.

5   Film is a medium which one would think natural for sign language users, but it is not often used for cultural purposes. If we contrast the attitude of the Deaf Americans who made the films of 1913 (like Veditz to whom we have already referred) with that of film making today, the difference becomes clear:

> From olden years, the masters of this sign language, the Peets, the Dudleys, the Elys, the Ballards are rapidly disappearing, and we, in

past years, loved these men. They had a precise command of sign language, they could communicate to us using only signs and we could understand them. But fortunately, we have several masters of sign language still with us. We want to preserve the signs as these men now use them to keep and pass on to future generations ... there is but one known means of passing on the language: through the use of moving picture films.

(Veditz, 1913)

Since then, there has been very little use of film for Deaf art, and the little that there has been, sees Sign and Deaf culture as almost incidental to the main purpose of the film (as you learnt in Unit 8). The early foresight of Veditz and people like him has been lost.

It is perhaps obvious that, if through the educational process one's language is devalued, then one's self-image becomes likewise devalued. In addition, deaf children's experience in education is that of being forced to focus on their imperfect speech, which further reinforces a sense of inferiority. Such a low self-image affects all areas of Deaf community life. After Deaf people in America marched to the Capitol in October, 1988 to demonstrate and enlist the help of Congress in establishing a Deaf president for the University of Gallaudet, Bob Johnson, a professor at Gallaudet, had this to say:

It is really remarkable because in all my experience I've seen deaf people be passive and accept the kind of treatment that hearing people give them. I've seen them willing, or seem to be willing, to be 'clients', when in fact they should be controlling things ... now all at once there's been a transformation in the consciousness of what it means to be a deaf person in the world, to take responsibility for things. The illusion has gone, and that means the whole nature of things can change for them now. I'm very optimistic and extremely enthusiastic about what I am going to see over the next few years. You know Tim Rarus—the one you saw at the barricades this morning, whose signing you so admired as pure and passionate—when he summed up in two words what this transformation is all about. He said 'Its very simple. No deaf president, no university', and then he shrugged his shoulders, looked at the T.V. camera, and that was his whole statement. That was the first time deaf people ever realised that a colonial client-industry like this can't exist without the client. It's a billion dollar industry for hearing people. If deaf people don't participate the industry is gone.

(Sacks, 1989)

This formed a sort of watershed where there was unequivocal recognition of their own power by the oppressed group. Accompanying this was a clear energizing insight into their responsibility to change the structures of the society. There are parallels with what Steve Biko was saying in his analysis of integration which powerfully questioned the supremacy of white leadership and white people as 'divinely appointed pace-setters in progress'. He was ultimately against 'the fact that a settler minority should impose an entire system of values on an indigenous people' (Biko, 1970). Here he was overturning the conventional ideas about the appropriate allocation of power, just as Johnson above is making clear that Deaf people are powerful, can call the tune and need not be at the mercy of how hearing people determine their lives. It has been the educational system which has created the dependency of clients. This is the first battle Deaf people have to overcome in their progress towards taking control of their own lives and determining the shape of the society. This sort of recognition marks the coming of a new age of potency of the movement.

1.6.3 Effects of oralism over time

In the literature you read about the manual/oral 'debate', but nowhere do you read of its results as experienced over time by people who have to live and work in the Deaf community. Here we describe some examples of how something that seems to outsiders merely to be about 'education', has social, cultural and linguistic effects.

(a) Deaf leadership

Any culture that wants to remain strong depends on the quality of its leadership. Even the emergence of leaders has been blocked by the way education has been arranged 'for' us. Since the Second World War, children who show the most potential for development have usually been educated at the Mary Hare Grammar School for deaf pupils, which has an oral policy. This has meant that some of our most able young people have been deflected from an exposure to our culture and our concern and so are unlikely to emerge as Deaf teachers. The growth of a political awareness of their role in the Deaf community has been stunted.

(b) Deaf club life

The passivity Johnson described even more strongly affects the running of Deaf organizations in the UK. In the USA, where since 1865 Gallaudet University produced able graduates, we find that the American National Association of the Deaf has always been run *by* Deaf people. In the UK, the British Deaf Association only had its first Deaf chairperson in 1983, and still has never had a full-time paid Deaf General Secretary.

The BDA became more politically active in the 1980s, but there are major problems in getting 'grass-roots' Deaf club members informed and involved. Video is costly and scarcely used, and the BDA's low income does not allow for a network of regional offices to spread information face-to-face. Yet in the Deaf community social information is extremely rapidly disseminated across the whole country. Oralism has not totally damaged this social aspect of culture. It has instead damaged the higher levels of cultural awareness, confidence and advocacy.

If leaders are prevented from emerging in school, where else would they develop? A natural possibility would be Deaf clubs. Some clubs are traditionally run by a two-tier structure. Deaf people run the 'Social Committee', and major decisions are taken by a Management Committee made up of local hearing notables, often with the Social Worker with Deaf People representing the social club's views for them. The continued unchallenged existence of such a structure reflects a lack of confidence of the local Deaf community. Within the clubs themselves, the levels of mutual support for each other have weakened. You have seen the views of older Deaf people about this in Unit 4. Younger people feel, in turn, excluded by older people. Deaf people with disabilities also receive inadequate support from the average Deaf person. Such a person, not surprisingly, has only negative feelings about speech and hearing aids, and has negative feelings about other Deaf people, usually younger people, who use speech. Since the latter 'hard of hearing' people often have more use of English, the club's rejection of their talents further restricts its growth.

Thus Deaf clubs changed from being started by Deaf people to being run by the local welfare officer for the Deaf. Someone had to try and hold things together. Nevertheless, as each generation saw further decline, it came to be perceived that Deaf people were pathologically incapable: social work cases rather than a community. These workers and the national organizations formed the bridge to modern society; it was they who had to educate the wider world about Deaf people and the Deaf community. It becomes clearer, therefore, that people who had a low image of Deaf people would reinforce that view in society, and the Deaf community would, therefore, not get the assistance it needed.

(c) Sign language interpreters

Central to any involvement of a language group in wider society is the existence of interpreters. As you learnt in Unit 7, in the UK the majority of interpreting occurring under oralism came from social workers to their 'clients'. Public interpreting was rare for much of this century. Yet once it started to emerge in the 1980s, meeting after meeting of hearing people at all levels, from by-election rallies to union meetings to ordinary social gatherings, found themselves transfixed by the 'signer' at the side of the room. Even if nothing at all was said by the Deaf person, those in attendance became much more interested in Deaf people and developed ideas to involve them more in their groups.

ITQ

If there had been interpreters everywhere for the last 100 years instead of the last 5 years, what do you think might have been different?

Widespread and long-term use of interpreters would have established sign language as the rightful and acceptable means of communication for Deaf people in the same way as Braille is the acceptable means of 'written' communication for blind people. Such access to information and ideas would have had a major impact on the lives of Deaf people. Moreover, it is inconceivable that oralism and oral approaches would have continued to have the major role that they do in the education of deaf children.

If anyone doubts that oralism is instrumental in limiting the use of interpreters, it is useful to remember an example from Holland, where the establishment of interpreters on television met with protests, from the Dutch teachers and parents of Deaf children, that signing would make Deaf people lazy, and that they should be trained to lip-read the television!

Similarly, in the UK, BBC's News Review's signer was removed in 1970. The main impetus for this was the argument from the hard-of-hearing population that sign language was no help to them and subtitles would be of more use. However, there were also some protests from oral deaf and from hearing people that signing was unsightly. The place of sign language interpreters remains an issue today in discussions of the new Broadcasting Bill (see Unit 10).

(d) Theatre, television and film

Access to the theatre and to television and film has been almost non-existent for most of this century. Yet if a climate which valued sign language had existed, much more would have been on offer in these fields. In the USA, by contrast, the value of Sign is continually reinforced by the activities of the National Theatre of the Deaf.

(e) Further and higher education and employment training

A major problem for Deaf people in the UK is the lack of a university or a further and higher education centre for the Deaf like Gallaudet University in the USA. Again it is not hard to imagine that the situation would be very different had Sign and sign language interpreters been accepted and provided by authorities, and if deaf literacy had not declined.

(f) Employment

It is abundantly clear that if Deaf education had been better and more extensive, the quality of employment for Deaf people would be greatly improved and the self-fulfilment and confidence arising from that would have fed back into the Deaf community and strengthened it. Having Deaf people in positions of responsibility and power would not only be important from the role model point of view but would have had strategic implications for the movement.

(g) Public support and interest

Deaf people, as we have seen, believe that the more society sees sign language, especially in status-valued places, the more interest there will be in learning it and in getting to know its users. This seems to be confirmed in the resurgence of Deaf people and Sign in the recent past. The tremendous demand to learn BSL had much to do with the prominence of Sign on television, and with plays like *Children of a Lesser God*. You may wonder just how many hearing people might have learned to sign, and how much Sign there would be on television and film, if oralism had not previously pushed it all underground.

(h) Oralism affects access to political awareness and alliances

All of us in society have our informational sources carefully controlled. Our education system teaches us what it wants us to know. The newspapers are owned by a select few, and represent only their views. Television is more complex, but as books like *Bad News* show, the doctoring of information is so deeply ingrained as to be almost unconscious on the part of those who shape it.

Dissenting views arise from people talking to each other and spreading that shared information, verbally or in writing. Deaf people are mostly cut off from these informed sources. They have to make sense of the world almost solely on surface data, having little access to spoken conversation or books. People use shared information to press for changes in their living conditions. As a result, for example, we no longer have such oppressive working terms and conditions, we have a national health service and unemployment benefits. Cut off by oralism from such processes, Deaf people have little idea about such basic social and political dynamics. There are many stories, for example, of Deaf people crossing picket lines unaware of the issues. Thus they are unaware of the possibility of using such processes to improve their own situation.

(i) Deaf 'role' models

Society's view of Deaf and disabled people is also shaped by the kind of people presented to them by those experts who have the power to mediate between these people and society. Thus we find a close relationship between oralists, and the kind of Deaf people chosen to 'prove' their theories. Many, like Nigel in the article by Paddy Ladd that you read earlier, are born with a partial hearing loss but can speak quite well. Harlan Lane's book *When the Mind Hears* also gives many examples, including some relating to the visits arranged in connection with the Milan Congress where it seemed that some of the demonstrations had been 'rigged'. The effects of this sort of false presentation of Deaf people is two-fold:

1   The effect on society is to continue to reinforce a particular view of deafness. Thus Jessica Rees received wide-scale publicity for her cochlear implant, and had published her autobiography in her early twenties (Rees, 1983). Similarly, the deaf actress Elizabeth Quinn got much publicity for her speaking role in the play *Hedda Gabler* in 1989. Stories about deaf children learning to speak, sing and play music are common. Recently, there has been a whole South Bank Show devoted to a deaf timpanist.

2   The direct effect on Deaf culture is that these people have in the past been held up by organizations for the deaf as the type of people they wish to support and often put in positions of power over Deaf people. These people usually speak and have 'useful hearing'. If they sign at all, they use Signed English and are actively hostile to the re-emergence of BSL.

Often they are people who became deaf, or who come from upper-middle class families with useful contacts. This results in an oralist-created sliding scale of values where hard-of-hearing people are seen as more intelligent and valuable than 'deaf and dumb' people. The effect of this is not just to divide the Deaf community and reduce Deaf people's confidence—what also happens is that these people set the agenda for all Deaf people in their contact with society.

(j) Type of people attracted to Deaf work

Within the political movement of Deaf activists oralism is seen as being clearly located in a right-wing ideology, and the rallying cries of the movement often underline the sinister shadows of fascism and selective eugenics as being in some way implicated in oralism. Alexander Graham Bell's own analysis of oralism drew his views of selective eugenics and his evolutionary ideas of the survival of the fittest together:

> Natural selection, (the Darwinist term for the survival of the fittest) operating on the continent of Europe for more than a century, has brought about the survival of the pure oral method and the almost total extinction of the French system of signs. The verdict of time is therefore conclusive as to the superiority of the oral over the sign method ...
>
> (Bell, 1894, in Winefield, 1981)

A study carried out by Professor Musgrove at Manchester University between 1971 and 1973 aimed to examine the views of students in different disciplines, and to grade them along a scale from 'progressive' to 'reactionary' (Musgrove, 1974). Students of twenty-four different disciplines were tested, including, almost by chance, trainee teachers of the deaf. When the results were completed, the teachers were placed twenty-first out of twenty-four; that is, at the reactionary end of the scale.

The implications for Deaf culture of the prevalence of such views among those who work for them include:

1   Authoritarianism in the classroom and in the welfare services.

2   A copying, by Deaf people, of this model rather than following a co-operative model, leading to divisions and dissension in the Community. (Deaf activists have noted the Deaf community's over-keenness to criticize: Deaf people refer to that as the 'Deaf Way'. But where was it learned?)

3   Infantilization of Deaf people. This has been noted by many newcomers to deaf work. It has even been noted on Deaf television programmes, where 'See Hear' has been compared to 'Blue Peter' in its production values. 'See Hear' arose from an 'Open Door' programme which presented a powerful case for television programmes specifically for Deaf people. However, despite its origins in this campaigning series, 'See Hear' is now a magazine programme for deaf people that has a lighter approach. Allsop *et al.* (1990) have carried out some research analysing the sort of items included in 'See Hear' over 7 years (1981–87). They reported that, at a time when there was an explosion of awareness of Deaf people's language and culture, 'See Hear' showed fewer items about rights, culture and language (the inclusion of such items dropped from 25 to 14 per cent).

4   The concept of cures: no one can easily pretend that blind people should be made to see nor mobility-impaired people to walk, but the idea persists that Deaf people can miraculously be taught to hear, or to speak. This affects the kind of people who choose to come into deaf work and continue the pattern from generation to generation.

There are many other effects that come from such a philosophy, and we are not saying that these views are held by all who work in the field. Indeed, the 1970s and 1980s saw more liberal and radical people enter the field. But, in the main, professional organizations are still influenced by the standard views and not by the new ones, so that, even as we write, there is no movement by teachers of the deaf to get Deaf people into teaching, or Deaf parents into the parents' organizations.

1.7 Working for change

You have learnt how oralism 'tightened the screws' through each successive generation: first as day schools were started; then as the partially deaf were sectioned off; through to the development of hearing aids, the establishment of Partially Hearing Units, and finally to mainstreaming and the use of cochlear implants. You have also learnt how oralism has resulted in low Deaf achievement, which in turn has led welfare workers to take more and more control over Deaf club life and national organizations. Each generation has seen a decline in the Deaf consciousness and ability of its young people, which could only be partly repaired by the culture. Thus by the 1960s and early 1970s, the crisis level within Deaf culture had risen to critical proportions. The tide had to turn.

But where were any signs of hope? The few Deaf activists were shut out of political positions by the last remnants of the old Missioners and welfare officers. The British Deaf Association, once set up to defend sign language in education, had become a focus for social aspects of culture, but not for moral, political or philosophical aspects. The Royal National Institute for the Deaf (RNID) positions seemed to be dominated by the deafened and the 'hearing-impaired', and the National Deaf Children's Society (NDCS) was largely a group for oral parents.

Change began at the BDA congress in 1974, as the delegates reaffirmed the importance of the education issue, and the organization began to produce regular pamphlets to influence the teaching profession and government bodies, and promoting leading Americans to tour the country in support.

In 1976 the NUD was formed as a Deaf-run organization, and immediately focused its attention on education. This led to an increased level of urgency in the campaign, as the NUD adopted tactics not seen in the Deaf community for many years, such as giving out leaflets at meetings; putting questions from the floor; picketing oralist meetings; and giving talks around the country to raise Deaf people's confidence and to put Deaf views to parents and teachers. Not constrained by charity membership, the NUD raised the tone and language level of the debate, and as those involved were Deaf themselves, perfectly complemented the BDA's more professionals-oriented approach. The NUD also used the concept of political alliance, in particular with the Scottish Workshop with the Deaf (who themselves combined Deaf and professional talents to achieve success in Scotland ahead of the rest of the UK).

Schools began to change to Total Communication quite rapidly between 1976 and 1982. It seemed that the corner had been turned. But then along came integration policies. For years, Partially Hearing Units had been growing in numbers: what the 1981 Education Act did, however, was to give official approval to such an idea, and thus to encourage the placement of profoundly deaf children in these units. Mainstreaming has grown so that 80 per cent of 'hearing-impaired' children are now in ordinary schools, despite the vehement protests of Deaf organizations on behalf of some of these children.

Although the 1981 Education Act was passed by able-bodied people, it has been supported by the majority of organizations involving people with disabilities. These too have ignored the protests of Deaf people, and thus blunted their lobbies. Earlier you heard the view that Deaf people felt that they were not disabled. With the clash over integration, the divisions have become very marked. Despite this, little change has been seen in disabled people's attitudes. The following is taken from a recent book written by a disabled woman aimed at schoolchildren and about children with special needs:

We all go to Assembly in a big hall where the head teacher talks to us. Next to her is a woman who translates everything she says into sign language for the children who cannot hear at all. It is very beautiful and I was a bit upset when I realised I could not control my hands enough to do it very well.... We usually sing in assembly and the deaf children often get fed up, but they do poems and stories in sign language for all of us and we love that.

(Mason, 1989)

This serves to illustrate that even disabled people themselves do not understand the consequences of integrated education for deaf children and the way it isolates them and cuts them off from their own culture. This is regrettable as it would be possible to form creative alliances and working partnerships with disabled people as another minority oppressed group if only there were this basic understanding of difference in the first place.

This idea was re-stated recently on television:

I think that disabled people at the moment are maybe making the mistake of saying 'How can we involve deaf people in our movement?' ...

... At the same time, deaf people have their own movement and are doing very well ... I think there is a need for disabled people to get involved in deaf people's campaigns. Learn the language, take interpreters along with you ... So there is integration both ways. But, as far as deaf people are concerned, the language is the key, that is the important thing.

(Transcription from M. Woolley on ITV 'Link', January 1990)

How, then, can the deadlock be broken?

You have already learnt how Deaf people define themselves as a linguistic minority group. Given the perceived urgency of the situation in education, the question becomes one of how to get political forces to accept this definition, despite all the media attitudes and resistance to Deaf people that we have heard about during the course and upon which we have particularly focused here.

The move the NUD made to the United Nations was followed by a decade of increased political activity, particularly by the BDA who began to publish manifestos, and to use stronger language involving the concept of human rights. Most crucially, they used a different philosophical approach, based around attaining recognition for BSL first, then asserting the educational implications of that recognition when 'the fish was hooked', as it were.

The NUD's attempts to get the World Federation of the Deaf to take up its responsibilities and negotiate with the UN did not bring immediate results, but the BDA used its initiative to set up a European zone of the WFD and from this to get a consensus of policies and rights from Deaf national organizations. The policies and rights advocated were then presented to the European Parliament and in 1988 the first stage towards EEC recognition of the national sign languages took place. Again, education was 'slipped in' as part of the package.

The BDA also involved Deaf people in a major lobby of Parliament in 1983. The issue was one that came from the disabled movement, for an anti-discrimination Act, but the high turn-out of Deaf people showed that such a political tactic was viable.

Two other tactics were employed by the BDA in the 1980s. The first, the setting up of interpreters and Deaf observers at party political conferences, opened up access for behind-the-scenes lobbying by Deaf people. The second was the establishment, with the NUD, of the Deaf Broadcasting Campaign in 1979. In going on to develop the work further themselves, Deaf people learnt to use tactics like picketing, lobbying and attention-grabbing media stunts for the first time. Nevertheless, the UK still lagged behind other European countries, such as France, Spain and Italy, which had had major marches, sit-ins and even hunger strikes, on issues of language and education.

The main tactics in the education field involved fighting the deaf school closures that began as a result of mainstreaming. At first there was some success, but there was no consistent national leadership to co-ordinate the actions, and more schools closed later in the 1980s. Then in 1985 the International Congress on Deaf Education came to Manchester. This gave Britain's Deaf activists the chance to change the resolution of the Milan Congress. The NUD and the radical region of the BDA, the North West Regional Council, organized a full range of tactics—putting banners round the city, organizing an alternative congress (as in Paris in 1900) and fringe meetings, and a press conference got them coverage not only on radio but also even on BBC Television's 6 O'Clock News.

Yet none of this turned the tide. In 1987, the NUD organized a linking up with the BDA, and allies at the Universities of Bristol, Leeds and Durham to oppose the government's new proposals for the training of teachers of the deaf. A one-hour television drama documentary 'Pictures in the Mind' was shown on Channel 4. To tie the two events together, the NUD persuaded Harlan Lane to come over from the USA and do a tour of Britain, which the BDA organized. The NUD then worked with a professional lobbyist to attract media coverage, focusing on the first ever Deaf picket of the Department of Education and Science, when both Harlan Lane and the director of 'Pictures in the Mind', Nigel Evans, were able to speak to the press. In terms of publicity, and thus to get support from the public, this was the most successful step yet.

From there, the obvious next step was to meet with the DES, and for the first time Deaf people presented in person their century-old case to those responsible. Unfortunately, as you may have guessed from the quotation taken from extracts of the official minutes, given in Section 1.6.1, very little was conceded by the DES in the three meetings which followed between them, the NUD and DEAF (Deaf Education Action Forum—a group set up by BDA members who were impatient with the lack of progress on the issue).

Since then, little more has happened. In 1990 a Deaf man, Clark Denmark, became the first Deaf person to be the BDA's Education Officer, and hopes were raised that a sustained national campaign might finally be possible.

We have discussed tactics as they have related to outward political action. But the 1980s were equally important for the rise in attention devoted to developing internal pride and confidence.

It is impossible to underestimate the impact of BSL recognition on the Deaf community. The work done in this field at the University of Bristol, and at Moray House College, Edinburgh, gave a boost to Deaf pride and confidence that simple political lobbying for issues such as better jobs could not do. Once the language was validated, Deaf people themselves became validated, and the same pattern of validation applied with the recognition of Deaf history by Lane's book (Lane, 1984).

Although the 'is BSL a language?' debate raged (and still rages) in the Deaf community, enough Deaf people, especially those who were children of Deaf parents, awoke to their inner potential, and the credit goes to the tactics of the British Sign Language Training Agency (BSLTA) based at the University of Durham. The then Director, Clark Denmark, undertook a tour of Britain, speaking in Deaf clubs to explain the work of BSLTA, and the importance of language and culture. One should not be surprised to learn that face-to-face contact is the best political tactic to use in the Deaf community, since BSL is not a written language. But no one had tried this approach on so wide a scale as this, and it threw up questions, some of which are discussed by Clark Denmark in his article in Reader Two.

The BSLTA then ran courses to train people to become BSL teachers, and many Deaf people gained their first educational qualifications in this way. Many of them were also 'ordinary' Deaf people, at the 'grass-roots' level and the BSLTA's success in reaching them has provided the basis for further successes in the 1990s.

◀ Reading
You should now re-read Article 6.7, 'British Sign Language Tutor Training Course' by A. Clark Denmark in Reader Two. ◀

There have been internal tensions between Deaf people who wanted to build on their pride in their language and culture and the Deaf political activists. The former focused on getting jobs held by hearing people in the deaf world, and stressing the importance of Deaf values and internal 'Deafness'. The latter included many Signed English users, who, although many accepted BSL, wanted the focus to remain on outward action.

This internal/outward issue remains to be resolved in the 1990s, as does the issue of the role of hearing people in the struggle. The NUD established a model of Deaf people acting for themselves, with hearing people becoming *allies* and using their expertise behind the scenes instead of acting as protectors. BSL research units followed this pattern to some extent; likewise the Deaf Broadcasting Campaign. The influence of the 1960s, of the 1970s' campaigns in education, and the 1980s' 'See Hear' television programmes, all saw more liberal hearing people enter the Deaf world and become valuable allies. However, there remained resentment of hearing people amongst some of the 'old guard', and with the emergence of BSL-focused supporters, new levels of tension developed as they became more aware of Deaf history and what had happened over time. The issue of hearing people's role thus becomes again one of internal focus versus outward action, for the 1990s to resolve.

As yet, there is still no real forum for discussion of Deaf political issues. Written (English) publications exclude many Deaf people, the journal *British Deaf News* focuses on BDA activity, and video is not yet used in this way. The creation of a discussion forum is a crucial political tactic which not only develops awareness and possible course of action, but also helps to bring people together to feel part of an on-going development in history and a coherent group. Small but vital starts to establish such a forum were made first by the Tribune Group in Lancashire, and the 1880 Committee in London. What they have shown is that 'out there' there are now significant numbers of Deaf people ready to take politically active steps. All that is lacking is leadership, both from the platform and from the national organizations.

To conclude this tale, it may seem that all roads lead to whatever action the BDA learns to take. As the only large organization *of* the Deaf (the NUD being only a small pressure group), it follows naturally that the British Deaf community is only as healthy as the BDA is healthy. But as Deaf people's confidence and determination continues to grow, if the BDA does not grow likewise, there is a real 'danger' that Deaf people will turn to other organizations for the kind of progress required. And since the BDA is the only Deaf organization elected from the grass roots up to national level, turning to other bodies would be damaging for the concept of a united community with an elected Deaf leadership.

2 A political analyst's tale

2.1 Minority groups and the political process

A minority group can become effective politically if it sees itself not as 'flawed' or 'different' or 'inadequate' within the general community but rather as having its own standing and an ability to bring about social change on its own behalf. Defining oneself as Deaf confers *a sense of belonging*—a significant move from being an individual Deaf person to becoming part of a collective. Here this process of alignment is scrutinized, together with the ways in which society disrupts this identification with the group in the case of Deaf people.

2.2 Defining oneself: Deaf people's definitions of themselves

The Activist's Tale outlined how Deaf people define themselves. This is perhaps an unusual perspective in that one rarely thinks of personal identity in that way; yet in subtle ways we do define ourselves by what we do, who our friends are, where we put our energies, the alliances we form and where we seek recognition. Sometimes we define ourselves through conflict—deciding what we are not, what we will put up with, what we will not be a party to or collude with. In this way we establish who we are, where we have been and where we are going. This is a fundamental step of the political process. Sometimes, however, it is blocked.

The *devaluing of personal experience* is a means by which society acts to disrupt and subtly discredit the growth of a political movement. The consequences of devaluing experience and thereby locating problems as personal misfortunes, individual failure to cope etc., produces *fragmentation* of activity. In all minority groups there is often a dearth of direct information about members' feelings, wishes and direct experience. A political awakening is often heralded by a crop of literature recounting experiences. Disabled women, for instance, as a minority group have long been cut off from 'mainstream society' and the women's movement itself. As they start to become active a whole new literature emerges about their experiences, written by them from their perspective. A similar new literature has marked the emergence of other movements, such as Black consciousness and gay liberation. In the case of the Deaf community we have heard how oralist education and mainstreaming have served to stifle such accounts of personal experiences by taking away or interfering with the natural means of communication.

The preceding account of the growth of the social and political movement of Deaf people has taken further some of the themes raised in Unit 8 by examining what constitutes *legitimate knowledge* on the basis of Deaf people's information and experiences rather than those of the professional service providers. The legitimation of common experiences by the group has been vital for the Deaf community as a political movement. If experiences are seen as individual then it is easy to conceive of problems experienced by that individual deaf person as *their* problem, *their* needs and *their* handicap. But if they are recognized as common experiences, then the focus of the problem can be shifted from the individual to society. This *shift of focus* is a vital part of the political process.

At the moment, a concern, arising partly from the new left, with 'equality of opportunity' has energized many professionals, administrators and politicians to make decisions about underprivileged and marginalized groups on the basis of little, if any, direct experience, data, or real understanding of their situation. It is a familiar story for Deaf people and minority groups, and over the years such administrative 'fashions' have stimulated political activity.

2.3 Unity, responsibility and the Deaf people's movement

2.3.1 Unity

The social status of being Deaf can create a serious disincentive to identify oneself as a Deaf person, to align with other Deaf people and act collectively on that basis. Similar to the way women in positions of power take on aspects of male identity, for many Deaf people, taking on power inevitably seems to involve taking on the trappings of the hearing world. It has been argued that deaf organizations in the UK do not run on policies developed at a grass-roots level but on policies formed at a higher level. Activists within the political movement of Deaf people claim such policies oppress Deaf people. Making decisions without consulting the grass roots of Deaf people is regarded as being a 'hearing' way of doing things even within deaf associations. The British Deaf Association has one of the best democratic structures and a much more widespread membership than any group of disabled people or foreign deaf groups. Unfortunately, it has not got the money to develop staffing posts to link Headquarters with the grass roots. Because these links are missing, questions arise about political 'correctness' which serve to underline the basic issue about alignment with the movement. Inevitably, suspicions and distrust can fragment a movement from the inside. The lack of money is a consequence of the lack of public interest in deafness. In the UK, deaf organizations such as the BDA are seen as charities; that is, as organizations 'doing good' to disadvantaged people rather than as political movements.

The development of unity forms the cornerstone of any effective minority political movement. The Black consciousness movement in South Africa illustrates this fundamental aspect of unity in the struggle to overthrow the oppression of apartheid. They worked towards a principled unity. Their definition of 'blackness' deliberately excluded those who were considered part of the system and those who were engaged in various forms of participation in government-conceived schemes. This was their definition of political correctness, appropriate alignment and principled unity. Such black people who colluded with the system were referred to as 'non-whites' because they accepted for themselves the negative definition and racial inferiority that formed the basis of government policy, but not before strenuous efforts had been made to dislodge them from their activities and the acceptances that set them apart from the people's struggles.

Within the minority group of Deaf people, therefore, similarly searching questions are raised about alignment and, with those, of course, questions about the robustness of the individual's resistance to oppression. From the outside these questions look like petty quarrels but they are fundamental to the unity of the movement. The ways in which Deaf people have defined themselves as Deaf, have embraced their own language and culture and mobilized politically around this recognition of identity is a crucial part of the life and power of Deaf people today.

Looking at the movement it seems that, in the most recent era of Deaf resurgence, there are those who:

(a) think it is enough just to be Deaf, they do not have to do anything such as committing themselves to the movement, they can just ride to power on the back of 'Deaf' resurgence;

(b) seem to think that being Deaf justifies any anti-hearing attitude towards others;

(c) behave negatively to any deaf person who, although not fully Deaf, is working towards social change.

The group, therefore, has a considerable way to go to achieve full unity.

2.3.2 Responsibility

Stereotyped beliefs about the limited mental capacities of deaf people and the inferior status regularly assigned to them have had a considerably negative effect on the self-confidence and self-esteem of deaf people. This is a typical phenomenon of oppression, and what happens is that the 'defect' spreads (Goode, 1978, in Baker-Shenk, 1986; Higgins, 1980). Negative stereotypes arise around the original differentiating characteristics, or, as they are popularly seen, 'defects'. People who are 'black' encounter an already negative stereotype which denotes beliefs about them being lazy, intellectually inferior and irresponsible. Similar generalizations have been made about deaf people being not very bright, mentally slow and so on. This view finds expression in comic stories about deaf people, similar to the 'Paddy' jokes about the Irish. The clinical and educational literature is replete with further negative stereotypes—deaf people being described as dependent and lacking in empathy (Althusser, 1974, in Baker-Shenk, 1986), as immature, rigid rather than flexible, exploitative of others, and abusive of relationship (Hurwitz, 1967, in Baker-Shenk, 1986), as egocentric, easily irritable and impulsive (Levine, 1956). Such negative views of deaf people have a powerful effect on undermining their confidence. There is an *internalization of oppression,* whereby a person starts to believe what is being said, thought and written about them. Recognizing low morale for what it is and identifying its causes has galvanized the various oppressed movements into confronting and challenging the stereotypes (the Irish 'jokes' being challenged, for example, as racist). It has also energized work and activities to promote, publicize and underline in every available forum the value, strengths, particular skills and abilities of members of those marginalized groups—the 'Black is beautiful' paradigm. This unit demonstrates how hard, in the case of deaf people, that struggle (the 'Deaf is who we are') has been, and how intransigent many agents of oppression have continued to be.

If defining oneself is a vital step in political activity, it entails throwing off internalized oppression. It is very hard indeed to identify with the one characteristic that is most stigmatized and devalued by the society in which one lives. It is easier to identify instead with the oppressor. Bettelheim most powerfully illustrates this phenomenon in his accounts of the way in which some people incarcerated in concentration camps in the Second World War began to act like the guards who were ill-treating them, as one way of re-establishing feelings of power. Bettelheim bases his observations on his internment in Dachau and Buchenwald:

Old prisoners were therefore sometimes instrumental in getting rid of the 'unfit'—in this way incorporating Nazi ideology into their own behaviour … . Self-protection required elimination of the 'unfit' prisoners, but the way in which they were sometimes tortured for days by the old prisoners and slowly killed was taken over from the gestapo … . Old prisoners who identified themselves with the SS did so not only in respect to aggressive behaviour, they would try to acquire old pieces of SS uniforms. If that was not possible they tried to sew and mend their uniforms so that they would resemble those of the guards. The length to which prisoners would go in these efforts seemed unbelievable, particularly since the SS punished them for their efforts to copy SS uniforms … . The old prisoners' identification with the SS did not stop with the copying of their outer appearance and behaviour. Old prisoners accepted Nazi goals and values, too, even when these seemed opposed to their own interests. It was appalling to see how far even politically well-educated prisoners would go with this identification.

(Bettelheim, 1943)

Black people straighten their hair and 'talk White', women dress in 'powerful' suits, Deaf people act oppressively like hearing people towards other Deaf people by, for instance, ignoring the wishes of grass-roots Deaf people in their work and in the Deaf organizations. Literature emerging from the Re-evaluation Co-counselling movement advances the view that people only become oppressors because they have been oppressed themselves. Freire talks of an ambivalence between oppressed people's desire for freedom, seen in their expressions of resentment and even hatred toward the oppressor, and their desire to be like the oppressor, and calls this an 'existential duality' (Freire, 1970). New forms of democracy within oppressed marginalized groups call for creative ways of becoming powerful and effective without taking on the mantle and the behaviour of the oppressor. In the women's movement, for example, a suggestion is that women should work towards restructuring society, work and power and join constructively in men's attempts to find 'new ways of being men' (Cockburn, 1989).

An urgent responsibility that has been enthusiastically embraced within minority groups has been to educate their members about the nature of injustice and the way in which they are commonly diminished and oppressed. Thus establishing Deaf people as a power group begins not with educating hearing people about the issues, but with making Deaf people more aware of themselves as distinct individuals. The primary education begins *within* the group to raise awareness of the necessity, if a just society is to be achieved, to secure more power for themselves and so become self-determining. Creative and meaningful participation in the political process has to be fully understood. A responsibility of oppressed minority groups is to educate *their own members* about how to develop plans to change the order of things. Thus, Barney Pityana, in an introduction to Steve Biko's book of writings (1988 edition) said: 'Black consciousness is quintessentially about enabling and enhancing the people's participation in their own struggles'. If transformations of power are to be achieved then activities *within* a movement have to be undertaken to ensure that there is a full sharing of understanding. Power sharing within the group, the sharing of knowledge and expertise and the joint democratic determination of group goals, is part of the creation of an effective revolutionary movement.

2.3.3 A people's movement

Deaf consciousness has ushered in a new era of political awareness whereby Deaf people have begun to see themselves as oppressed people. The social and political movement for Deaf rights is in every sense a people's movement. It has helped Deaf people become more analytical and articulate about their lot. All the ramifications of Deaf culture—poems, writing, art, through sign language as rich and as expressive as any spoken language—have emphasized their distinct identity. There have also been public events as landmarks in the struggle, demonstrations and rallies, asserting Deaf people's aspirations.

As a people's movement the Deaf community has a long history. Discrimination has been systematic, widespread and sustained over a long period of time. Hearing people are often ill-informed about deafness and oblivious of the history of the Deaf community, perhaps even less informed than some educated people were two or three centuries ago. There is also indifference—the situation and history of Deaf people is not something people generally want to concern themselves with. It is the common lot of many marginalized groups: women, not too long ago, pointed out that history had largely neglected *her* story. The significance and exclusiveness of verbal language for social being and recognition is revealed by the history of Deaf people, a history we have followed earlier in the course.

The period from the late eighteenth to the middle of the nineteenth century was important in the growth of a people's movement, with the establishment of deaf schools staffed by Deaf teachers and various forms of sign language flourishing throughout the world, with the consequent emergence of Deaf people from isolation, despair and obscurity. This part of the collective history of Deaf people is documented by Harlan Lane (1984). Deaf people began to take on positions of responsibility becoming recognized as gifted and able citizens. The activities in Europe spread also to the USA and strengthened and reinforced activities there. As we have heard, aspirations became boundless.

Oralism, however, won its battle and sign language and Deaf teachers disappeared from Deaf education. The Congress of Milan of 1880 was a landmark in this change:

> Nevertheless, the meeting at Milan was the single most critical event in driving the language of the deaf beneath the surface, it is the single most important cause—more important than hearing loss—of the limited educational achievements of today's deaf men and women eighty per cent of whom in America are engaged in manual or unskilled labour.
>
> (Lane, 1984)

The location, organizers, officers, exhibitions and membership of the Milan Congress had, it seems, been carefully chosen to ensure an oralist outcome and some of the demonstrations were suspect.

Reference to this occasion has acted as a rallying cry to the political movement ever since, in that so few could have decided the fate of so many in a brief moment in history. It can be seen as providing the same sort of watershed for Deaf people as Clause 28 for gays, lesbians and their children. In effect, it turned Deaf people into an oppressed people. The issues of self-identity, unity, responsibility and the strength of the people's movement became real and urgent. For gay people, the turning point in 'coming out' was the perceived oppression of Clause 28. For Deaf people it might be argued that there is no choice.

Lane refers to 'the wave of pure oralism' which washed over Europe in the aftermath of Milan. As a result, Deaf people had actively to resist being identified as deficient hearing people in a world of sound. In terms of political processes, why did this happen when things seemed to be going remarkably well for Deaf people and their language? Lane describes the way that many people and schools were swept up in the advance of oralism:

> There is no single explanation for such tides in human affairs. I have cited the confluence of nationalism, elitism, commercialism, and family pride. Another contributing cause was the educators' desire for total control of their classrooms, which cannot be had if the pupils sign and the teacher knows none. The teacher then becomes the linguistic outcast, the handicapped. Nor can he or she acquire the necessary skill in a year, or even two, any more than an Anglophone teacher can so rapidly prepare himself to teach in French. The understandable reluctance of hearing teachers to master a language radically different from their own continues to have the greatest weight in what are represented as pedagogical discussions. There was a time when teachers of the deaf could not practice without a knowledge of their pupils primary language. But the vast expansion of schools in Europe and America created more professional positions than there were educators and administrators fluent in sign. Increasingly, people with few ties to the deaf community dominated their education.
>
> (Lane, 1985)

So Deaf people have a collective history and, in common with other minority groups, the history never has an end—there are always some underlying anxieties about difference waiting to be fuelled or fed. It was said that the Holocaust could never happen again, yet we now see the growth of anti-Semitism in Europe. So too, in this era when Deaf people's language and culture is coming to be widely recognized, we note the serious anxieties about mainstreaming and cochlear implants endangering the Community's future.

So the sweep of collective history which has brought us from the Milan conference to the integrated education debates of the present day has had its effect on how the Deaf person thinks, believes and aligns. This history tells a tale of a group of people marginalized by a society and by the interventions of that society, being rendered almost impotent in their comprehension of the political process and ways of countering oppression.

3 The end of the pilgrimage

We have read of the factors that combine to drive an oppressed minority group to 'take up arms' and fight for social change. We have followed the ways in which Deaf people's activities have paralleled the struggles of other marginalized or minority groups in the face of oppression. One might now ask, 'where does it all go from here'? Do these story tellers, as in Chaucer's *Tales*, end their 'pilgrimage' in Canterbury? Is changing the situation a matter of new legislation outlawing discrimination against a linguistic minority group and providing appropriate services for them? Would the destination, therefore, be most appropriately Westminster? Or are there infringements of human rights to freedom, to expression and to self-determination, to be referred to the Court of Human Rights in Strasbourg— or the United Nations? Moving from rhetoric into action seems the next crucial step in claiming power by the powerless. It was a politically astute step, therefore, by the NUD to approach the United Nations and to target their major activities there. Why was this so important? Could the United Nations really do anything to change things in the way the Deaf community wished? No, they probably could not, as the Charters and Conventions are very largely statements of intent rather than programmes of action. They outline in a broad sense how things should be, but do not specify who is responsible for delivering these visions. They have no executive power. They may meet with general approval and provide a warm glow but in practical terms they have no teeth. Nevertheless, they do represent significant statements of the climate of the times, they embody human aspiration. In starting at this level, therefore, the NUD was setting the case of the oppression of Deaf people in the boldest possible context, aiming at a vision of how the world should be. It also demonstrated something about the transformations that were happening in the movement, exemplified at Gallaudet more recently. It marked a coming of age of the movement. The Charter of Rights of the Deaf uses the language of oppression to political effect and aligns itself with pan-world visions of human conduct and dignity.

It is worth lingering on this point to grasp its full significance. Deaf people through this means were asking for their own group to be recognized as a distinct linguistic minority group—an identity for which they had fought long and bloody battles. The way they were going about trying to build the foundations of social change used the language and conventions of the hearing world to make their case, but on their own terms, not as 'clients'. They were skilfully arguing their rights as citizens of the social world to become enfranchised members, to be able to play a part in designing that world, and to have their rights to self-determination acknowledged and implemented.

Strategically it was a good move to bring pressure on the UK to amend its contractual obligations to meet the self-defined needs of Deaf citizens. With this in view the Charter moved from recommendation for action to a basis for legislative formulation with a clearly defined responsibility for safeguarding these rights. We referred earlier to the counterpoint between the theoretical and academic debates of the professionals in the 'debating chamber' and the rhetoric and struggles of Deaf activists in their movement for social change. This has served to sharpen the identity of Deaf people and make clear their objectives of self-determination.

Human rights relate to four areas of activity. There are 'rights' at the level of the international visions contained in manifestos etc. These are visions with no statement of who is responsible for realizing them. At the level of national government, however, it is possible to have statements of rights embodied in legislation with a clear allocation of responsibility and clear procedures to deal with infringement of rights. Thus a declaration of human rights becomes linked to an obligation to safeguard them. A third aspect of human rights concerns the responsibility of the community to empower a group to determine its own welfare and destiny. A fourth concerns the individual's rights to self-determination. We have seen in the history of Deaf people as a linguistic minority group the way in which their rights as a group, and consequently as individuals, have been eroded. Whatever the intention, the outcome has been that deaf people have felt that they have not received the services and support they need, that this is a violation of human rights and a failure of the machinery of government to safeguard these.

Suggestions for further reading

This unit has drawn together material from a number of different sources. If specific issues have been of particular interest to you, you may wish to follow up the references in the text on those issues.

In addition, the following two books, already used in the course, develop further themes raised by this unit:

LANE, H. (1984) *When the Mind Hears*, New York, Random House. (Also published by Penguin Books, 1988.)
This book is written by a hearing person from the viewpoint of Laurent Clerc, a deaf man who travelled from France to America in 1816. Through the device of providing an account of the life of Clerc, it describes many of the deaf people living in Europe and America in the nineteenth century and the issues that confronted them. These issues reverberate today and are discussed in this unit.

SACKS, O. (1989) *Seeing Voices*, London, Picador. (Published in paperback, 1991.)
Sacks, another hearing man, describes in this book his own explorations of the Deaf community and his discovery that Deaf people are 'people with a distinctive language, sensibility and culture of their own'. Among other things, he describes his own visit to Martha's Vineyard, and gives a first-hand account of the events at Gallaudet surrounding the protests at the election of a hearing president and the eventual choice of a deaf president.

References

ACTION ALLIANCE OF PARENTS OF THE DEAF (1986) *Report,* Fremont, CA, Action Alliance of Parents of the Deaf.

ALLSOP, L., WOLL, B. and SPENCE, R. (1990) 'Sign language varieties in British television', in Prullwitz, S. and Bollhaber, T. (eds) *Current Trends in European Sign Language Research,* Hamburg, Signum Press.

BAKER-SHENK, C. (1986) 'Characteristics of the oppressed and oppressor peoples: their effects on the interpreting contexts', in McIntyre, M. (ed.) *Proceedings of the Ninth National RID Convention, Interpreting: The Art of Cross Cultural Mediation,* RID Publications.

BELL, A.G. (1884) *Memoir Upon the Formation of a Deaf Variety of the Human Race,* Washington, DC, National Academy of Sciences.

BETTELHEIM, B. (1943) 'Individual and mass behaviour in extreme situations', *Journal of Abnormal and Social Psychology,* vol. 38, pp. 417–52.

BIENVENU, M.J. (1989) 'Disabled we are not', *TBC News,* no. 13, April.

BIKO, S. (1970) 'Black souls in white skins', in *SASLO Newsletter,* August. (Reprinted in Biko, 1988.)

BIKO, S. (1988) *I Write What I Like,* Harmondsworth, Penguin Books.

CARVER, R. (1988) 'Deaf culture; dying or changing', *TBC News,* September.

COCKBURN, C. (1989) 'Some thoughts on equal opportunity', Workshop of the European Forum of Socialist Feminists 4th International Conference, Manchester, 1988.

DENMARK, A. C. (1990) 'British Sign Language tutor training course', in Gregory, S. and Hartley, G.M. (eds) (1990) *Constructing Deafness,* London, Pinter Publishers. (D251 Reader Two, Article 6.7)

DESLOGES, P. (1779) 'Observations du'un sourd et muet sur "un cours élémentaire d'éducation des sourds et muets" ', in Lane, H. (ed.) *The Deaf Experience,* London, Harvard University Press, 1984.

DIMMOCK, A. (1980) 'Chairman's report to the Second Convention of the National Union of the Deaf', *Report of the Second Convention,* Guildford, National Union of the Deaf.

DIMMOCK, A. (1986) 'Chairman's report to the Fifth Convention of the National Union of the Deaf', *Report of the Fifth Convention,* Guildford, National Union of the Deaf.

EQUAL OPPORTUNITIES REVIEW (1989) 'Rastafarians protected by the Race Relations Act', *News,* no. 25, May/June.

FINKELSTEIN, V. (1990) ' "We" are not disabled, "you" are', in Gregory, S. and Hartley, G.M. (eds) (1990) *Constructing Deafness,* London, Pinter Publishers. (D251 Reader Two, Article 7.6)

FREIRE, P. (1970) *Pedagogy of the Oppressed,* New York, Seabury Press.

GREGORY, S. and HARTLEY, G. (eds) (1990) *Constructing Deafness,* London, Pinter Publishers. (D251 Reader Two)

HIGGINS, P. (1980) *Outsiders in a Hearing World: A Sociology of Deafness,* London, Sage Publications.

IBA (1984) *Annual Report,* London, Independent Broadcasting Association.

LADD, P. (1981) 'Making plans for Nigel: the erosion of identity by mainstreaming', in Taylor, G. and Bishop, J. (eds) (1990) *Being Deaf: The Experience of Deafness*, London, Pinter Publishers. (D251 Reader One, Article 10)

LANE, H. (1984) *When the Mind Hears*, New York, Random House. (Also published by Penguin Books, 1988.)

LANE, H. (1985) 'On language, power and the deaf', address to the Manchester Deaf Club, 7 August 1985.

LEVINE, E.S. (1956) *Youth in a Soundless World, A Search for Personality*, New York, New York University Press.

MASON, M. (1989) *Nothing Special*, London, Woking Press.

MUSGROVE, F. (1974) *Ecstasy and Holiness*, London, Methuen.

NASH, H.T. (1980) 'The bureaucratization of homicide', in Smith, D. and Thompson, E.P. (eds) *Protest and Survive*, Harmondsworth, Penguin Books.

NUD (not dated, circa 1982) *Charter of Rights for the Deaf. Part One, the Rights of the Deaf Child*, Guildford, National Union of the Deaf.

REES, J. (1983) *Sing a Song of Silence*, Kensall Press.

SACKS, O. (1989) *Seeing Voices*, London, Picador.

SMITH, D. and THOMPSON, E. P. (eds) (1980) *Protest and Survive*, Harmondsworth, Penguin Books.

TAYLOR, G. and BISHOP, J. (eds) (1990) *Being Deaf: The Experience of Deafness*, London, Pinter Publishers. (D251 Reader One)

VEDITZ, G.W. (1913) *Preservation of Sign Language*, film, Silver Spring, MD, National Association of the Deaf.

WASHABAUGH, W. (1986) *Five Fingers for Survival*, Ann Arbor, MI, Karoma.

WINEFIELD, R. (1981) *Bell, Gallaudet and the Sign Language Debate*, unpublished doctoral dissertation, Harvard University School of Education.

WOODWARD, J. (1982) 'Beliefs about and attitudes towards deaf people and sign language on Providence Island', in Woodward, J. (ed.) *How You Gonna Get to Heaven if You Can't Talk with Jesus*, Maryland, T.J. Publishers.

Acknowledgements

Grateful acknowledgement is made to the following sources for permission to reproduce material in this unit:

Figures

Figures 9.2, 9.3 The National Union of the Deaf, covers from issues 23 and 35 of the NUD Newsletter.

Grateful acknowledgement is made to Trevor Landell for permission to use his painting on the covers and title pages throughout the units of this course.

NUD.

BDA - hearing led

Deaf leaders = oral educ hearing ∴ into socieds

professional respected

Deaf role models.

Deaf

Medical model.

~ diagnose
Nor may Kn
BSL

Linguistic Minority — Educatn — oral
Admin model

mainstrea

Teacher of Deaf
don't need to Kn
BSL

deaf
accept
dual
role is
good for them

no forum
for Deaf pd
issues

Admin

Disability legislatn

disabled
covers up
lack of
resources.

Pg 54

Integratn
pd of state
+ church.

not an political agenda

Culture passed on at school

min group pd effectum = sense of worth
standing

developt of unity